Leading Groups

A Training Course

Leading Groups

A Training Course

MARGARET PARKER

EPWORTH PRESS

British Library Cataloguing in Publication Data

Parker, Margaret
    Leading groups: a training course.
    1. Church group work   2. Christian
leadership
    I. Title
    267   BV652.2
    ISBN 0–7162–0431–2

First published 1987
by Epworth Press, Room 195, 1 Central Buildings,
Westminster, London SW1H 9NR

Phototypeset by Input Typesetting Ltd, London
and printed in Great Britain by
The Camelot Press Ltd, Southampton

CONTENTS

INTRODUCTION

Why is this course needed?

Throughout the church there is a tremendous upsurge of interest in small groups. They appear in many different forms ranging from Bible studies to groups discussing how to bring up children, prayer fellowships to debates on topical issues, enquirers' meetings to theological study sessions. Different though they are, they have one thing in common – they are made up of people who want to grow in their understanding, experience and application of the Christian faith.

To be effective these groups need good leaders. Good leaders will be committed to the idea of small groups, they will have a deep love for God and a concern for their own and other people's personal growth, and will almost certainly feel the need for some training.

Hence this training course.

What is the course aiming to do?

The course is primarily designed to give guidance, ideas and encouragement to people training and helping group leaders in individual churches, circuits, dioceses or districts. Trainees could find it useful to have their own copies for future reference as the course contains an abundance of ideas for meetings as well as valuable information about group theory.

If necessary, individual group leaders may use the course on their own, although much of the benefit comes from the experience of participating in it with others.

How is the course structured?

There are eight suggested training sessions. They can be taken in any order, although there is some logic in the order in which they are presented here. If time is short, sessions can be merged; the approximate length of each session is given to assist the trainer with the planning.

The notes for each session are in two parts.

1. The preparatory reading for the trainer. The pages have a grey edge.
2. Detailed suggestions of how to present each session, including group exercises.

There is no copyright on Part 2 of any session; trainers are encouraged to give copies of the handouts to the trainees.

What else is provided?

The Appendix contains useful information on resources for leaders of groups. It is wide-ranging but not exhaustive.

2 *The example of Jesus Christ*

Jesus Christ gives us a precedent for working with small groups. He called the twelve to be with him (Mark 3) and spent a great deal of time with them. Some of his time was with a small group of three disciples (e.g. Matt. 17). We can learn a great deal from him and during the course we will note some of his styles and methods of leadership.

Seven practical points for trainers

1. *Number of trainees in a group*

A good number is about twelve (Jesus knew what he was doing!)

The smallest viable group for training is probably six. The biggest is however many the room will comfortably hold.

2. *When to hold the training course*

The course can start as soon as the trainer is ready, a group of trainees has been recruited and suitable dates selected.

Ideally the course will have eight separate sessions. These may be held one evening a week for eight weeks; some groups may prefer to have more than one session per week.

Sessions can be merged, or shortened to fit in with the times available.

Some groups will prefer to spend a whole Saturday on the course, or several Sunday afternoons.

If parents of young children are involved it may be possible to offer baby-sitting or crèche facilities.

3. *Where to hold the training course*

Find a venue which is convenient for the majority of the trainees and where there are adequate facilities, including provision of suitable refreshments, comfortable (but not too comfortable!) seats, space for any projectors and screens/whiteboard/flipchart/wall charts you wish to use, and adequate car parking.

4. *Publicity*

People will not come to the training course if they do not know it is being held!

The publicity may be undertaken by the trainer or preferably by another person who will act as secretary and promoter of the course.

Use every available means to spread the word: *Personal invitation* supported by written details is most effective.

Letters to priests or ministers, church stewards, deacons or wardens, secretaries of pastoral committees, and class and group leaders.

Information at church, circuit and district or diocesan meetings.

Posters in churches in the catchment area.

Handbills containing all relevant details to be distributed at every opportunity. (See page 4 for sample handbill for publicity).

Booking forms will encourage people to commit themselves to the course. A small charge to cover expenses may be acceptable. The booking form can include the question, 'What do you hope to gain from this course?' This will help the trainees to come to the course with specific expectations, and will help the trainer to know what they are expecting! If any of the expectations are unrealistic, the trainer will be able to talk this over with the trainee at the outset. (See page 4 for sample booking form.)

5. *Reading and personal preparation*

The trainer will read the course material and digest it. The training course is not a blueprint to be followed slavishly; it is a set of suggestions to be adapted according to local requirements, taking into account the skill and experience of the trainer, who will have personal preference on styles and methods.

There are several books for background reading on the theory and practice of group work. See Appendix for further reading.

In our personal preparation for training and leadership we will do well to follow the example of Jesus who often went away on his own to pray. All the skills, techniques, ideas and preparation in the world will be ineffective without the work of God in us, in the trainees, and in the members of the groups they will be leading. Pray for yourself and for them, that God will equip you and use you for the task he has given you.

6. *Preparing the presentation*

After the material in the preparatory reading for the trainer for each session has been digested, visual aids, handouts* and own notes need to be prepared.

A check-list of what to take to each session will be useful.

***Handouts** are to be given to the trainees. They may be summaries of a talk, with headings under which trainees can make their own notes. They may be instructions for group exercises. They may be points for discussion. Many handouts are included in this training course. Some trainers may prefer to prepare their own.

---

7. *Planning the first session*

- Make sure the room is warm and welcoming. If the course is being held at a church with which some of the trainees are not familiar, put up notices to indicate which rooms you are using, and if possible have someone to welcome people as they arrive.
- If the trainees did not fill in a booking form including the question, 'What do you hope to gain from this course?', give them the question on slips of paper as they arrive and ask them to be thinking about it. They can be asked to hand in their answers during or immediately after the session.
- A hand-made poster will help to brighten up the room and will provide a talking point.
- Plan to start at the advertised time with a welcome and any necessary practical details (such as where the loos are!) followed by opening devotions led by the minister or someone other than the trainer.
- Provide blank paper for the trainees to take notes. A plastic or cardboard folder for each trainee for notes and handouts will be useful.
- Formulate your aims for this course and be ready to explain them to the trainees.
  The aims will vary but may include:
  - to help group leaders to discover how people learn and how groups work;
  - to demonstrate how to set up a group;
  - to suggest ways of bringing vitality back into a group;
  - to suggest ways of dealing with problems;
  - to boost confidence through a deeper understanding of the role of the group leader;
  - to build up for later reference a file of methods, techniques, ideas and resources;
  - to share in the experience of being part of a learning group.

You, the trainer are now ready to launch out.

4   Sample handbill for publicity

Do you lead a small group, class meeting, Bible Study, or fellowship?
Or do you think that one day you might have to?

Then come and join us at a series of TRAINING SESSIONS

led by

at

on

from   until

cost

During the training sessions you will learn about the value of small groups in the church, different styles of leadership, how to set up a group, and how to deal with problems. There will be scores of ideas for meetings for your group. You can't afford to miss it!

Booking forms available from:

Sample booking form

BOOKING FORM FOR TRAINING SESSIONS FOR LEADERS OF GROUPS

to be held at

on

Name
Address

Phone
Church

Brief details of groups you have led, or lead now, or may lead in the future

What do you hope to gain from these sessions?

Signed

Please send this form with booking fee (   ) to:

SESSION ONE
The Value of Small Groups

Preparatory reading for the trainer

It is significant that churches which are seen to be alive and growing in both numbers and depth have small groups meeting week by week, usually in members' homes. We cannot be certain which is the cause and which is the effect; does the presence of small groups encourage church growth, or do growing churches encourage small groups? What is clear is that the two go together and group leaders need to be aware of the *value* and effectiveness of the small group.

The class meeting, small group, housegroup, homegroup, adult Sunday class, by whatever name we choose to call it, can meet people's needs both intellectual and emotional. In addition it can offer a relaxed setting in which Christians are able to share their faith with friends and neighbours; and it should be a springboard for action.

1. *The small group meeting intellectual and educational needs*

When communication is only *one way* there is no guarantee that what has been heard and understood is what the speaker intended. There is no opportunity for clarification or amplification.

An advantage of one-way communication is that more information can be delivered in a given time, and it must be said that the sermon has a central part to play in the life of the church; God speaks to us by his Holy Spirit through the words of the preacher. But which of us can honestly say that our minds have never wandered under the ministry of even the most effective preacher?

Jesus did not lecture his disciples, but enabled them to discover things for themselves, by taking them with him where he went – to heal the sick, to talk with enquirers, to mix with all kinds of people, to his transfiguration. For the disciples the group experience in the presence of Jesus was an education. There must have been plenty of discussion and Jesus answered their questions, which he had doubtless stimulated in their minds by who he was and what he said.

Discussion enables a leader to find out where people are in their thinking, and to start from there.

If we are to grow in understanding of Christian truth we need opportunity for *dialogue, discussion, conversation* and *participation*. It has been said that our churches are places for meetings, rather than meeting; that is, the productive meeting of minds and hearts.

6   Small groups provide opportunities for people:

- to learn at their own pace
- to seek clarification when necessary
- to spark off thoughts in each other's minds
- to develop their ideas by putting them into words
- to share and explore ideas with others
- to challenge each other's assumptions, and to be challenged
- to be stimulated and helped to concentrate because of the variety of voices.

To be useful, group discussion needs some input, otherwise the meetings will merely be a sharing of ignorance. Good leaders will ensure that facts and not just opinions are expressed and they will be able to draw out from the members of the group points which will move the discussion on. They will not see themselves as the fount of all knowledge nor feel the need to impart all information themselves.

2. *The small group meeting psychological and emotional needs*

We see Jesus as the leader who gave his disciples a valuable group experience which helped to meet their emotional needs. He accepted them just as they were: he had no illusions about them, but he loved them and he saw their potential. By bringing them together he helped them to accept each other and gave them a sense of belonging.

If our emotional needs are to be met, we need a sense of belonging and a feeling of being accepted. The small group can provide this.

It can offer a sense of personal value and worth;

it can engender mutual respect and a building up of healthy and helpful relationships;

it can lead to personal growth and self-awareness and a deeper understanding and acceptance of other people's thoughts and feelings.

In addition to the pastoral care the leader will give to the group members, the members themselves can offer each other care and support, and help to meet each other's needs.

In short, the small Christian group at its best will offer to the members a caring and supportive environment suitable for promoting the wholeness sought by every Christian.

3. *The small group as a base from which to share our faith*

In the natural and relaxed atmosphere of a home people talk about whatever is important to them. Where better, then, to share our Christian faith? Questions can be asked, large subjects explored, deep issues raised, misconceptions removed and new ideas adopted in this informal and non-threatening environment.

It is helpful to use the homes of the least committed people, as they need to feel as comfortable as possible, and provided they are happy to welcome a few others into their home, they will benefit from the security this gives them. The visitors will need to be prepared to listen to what everyone says. It's important to keep the lines of communication open and ensure a second visit!

If people see that we can talk naturally and honestly about our faith, our God and our church, not pretending to know all the answers, but telling of what God has done in our lives, they may want to know more. They will probably not initially come to church but by using the small group method, we can take the gospel to them.

4. *The small group as a springboard for action*

Our aim is not only to foster the growth of the members in understanding, experiencing and sharing their faith, but also to enable them to apply it in daily living. If the regular meeting of small groups does not lead to some changes in attitudes and actions it is probably not working well. The meeting of people should not be seen as an end in itself but as a means to an end. It may lead to:

- regular visiting of an elderly neighbour
- joining the Samaritans
- selling Tearcraft produce
- writing to MPs about issues arising in parliament
- working with Amnesty International
- joining the local council or Parent-Teacher Association
- adopting an unwanted child
- forming a mother and toddler club
- mending equipment for the Youth Club
- engaging in systematic Christian studies
- becoming a local preacher or reader
- knitting blankets for Oxfam
- welcoming people in the church porch
- or a thousand and one other things!

Clearly not all members of the group will engage in the same activities, although there is value in a shared project arising out of for instance a Bible study, where members feel motivated together to take action. In individual activities members will encourage each other and support each other in prayer and by showing continuing interest. If all in the group have seen the need for something to be done, and some of the group are the obvious people to do it, they will need the moral support of the others.

Groups have these four purposes.
(i) To meet intellectual and educational needs.
(ii) To meet emotional and psychological needs.
(iii) To be a base from which to share faith.
(iv) To be a springboard for action.

If any one of the four is missing there is a need to take a close look at the way the group functions. See session two for how a group functions.

Presentation of the session

The opening session of the training course will have three parts.

Summary

1. Welcome and opening devotions, and aims of course
2. Warming-up exercises or ice-breakers*
3. Thinking about the value of small groups including group exercises.

---

*Warming-up exercises or ice-breakers are designed to break down barriers which exist when a group first meets. The exercises help group members to get to know each other and feel comfortable together, after which they are more ready to work together.

---

1 and 2 are unique to the opening session. 3 sets the pattern for subsequent sessions, with the presentation of the material given in the preparatory reading for the trainer, followed by group exercises.

1. Welcome and opening devotions, and aims of course

For details see Introduction (page 3) on planning the first session.

2. Warming-up exercises

Use either or both of these. You will need to judge their appropriateness.

(*a*) *Complete the sentences*

Aims: To make people confident and relaxed as they complete a simple assignment.
   To give insights into what works well and what can go wrong in a group.
You will need: two slips of paper for each trainee
   re-usable adhesive or drawing pins
   large wall chart headed 'The best . . .'
   large wall chart headed 'The worst . . .'
   See page 12 for explanation of wall charts.

Method: Hand out two slips of paper to each trainee. One will say 'The best small group meeting I attended was good because. . . .' The other will say 'The worst small group meeting I attended was bad because. . . '
   Give trainees about three minutes to complete the two sentences. They will then attach their completed sentences to the wall charts under the appropriate heading, with drawing pins or re-usable adhesive. They do not need to put their names on the slips.

Depending on the time available, either read out all the completed sentences, or give opportunity for trainees to look at them.

The trainer should note the thoughts expressed on the slips for use in session two. Brief comments will suffice for now.

(b) *Ball of string*

Aims: To introduce trainees to each other by name and to illustrate the random criss-cross nature of discussion in the small group, with some people dominating and others overlooked.

Do not explain the second aim to the trainees, or else they will ensure that no one gets the string more often than the others, and that no one is missed out. The aim is to illustrate what *does* easily happen rather than what *should*.

You will need: One ball of thick string.

Method: Sit in a tight circle of up to twelve people. In large groups either have several balls of string and several circles, or ask for twelve volunteers. The trainer is one of the twelve. The leader holds an end of the ball of string and tosses the ball to someone else who then tosses it to another person, each holding on to a bit of the string. This continues so that a criss-cross pattern of string is formed. People call out their names when they receive the ball of string.

Stop the exercise when you feel the point has been made, or when the string runs out!

This can cause great hilarity, and the atmosphere should be kept light and relaxed.

Take the string out of the way and explain that that was just a bit of fun, but that it illustrates how conversation can flow in a discussion.

Refer to this exercise in session three when talking about styles of leadership.

3. *Thinking about the value of small groups*

This is the main part of session one. The preparatory reading for the trainer provides the ideas.

In advance
 (i) Prepare four wallcharts or overhead projector transparencies, as shown on page 10. See page 12 for explanation of wallcharts and overhead projectors.
(ii) Make copies of the Value of Small Groups on page 11 as handouts for trainees.

At the session
 (i) Explain that it is important for class leaders, housegroup leaders, leaders of all small groups to understand the value of what they are doing. This session is aimed at giving that understanding.

 The small group can be seen to have a four-fold value, and we will be looking at all four aspects.
(ii) Use either wallcharts or transparencies to show the four aspects of the value of small groups. Take them one at a time, and talk about them, filling in the right hand side of the chart as you go along. Draw out ideas from trainees where possible, and use their wording on the charts.

 Some discussion will probably follow, and trainees should be encouraged to express their views, but not reminisce at any length!
(iii) When all four charts are filled in, give the trainees the handout from page 10 and allow time for them to fill in the details on the right hand side. Alternatively, provide copies of page 11 as a handout, with the points already included. This will save time but will not necessarily be an accurate record of what has been said in your training course.

1. *Meet educational needs*

2. *Meet emotional needs*

3. *Give opportunities for sharing faith*

4. *Are a springboard for action*

1. *Meet educational needs*	Two way communication Participation Discussion Opportunities for questions and clarification Progress at suitable pace sparking off ideas from each Inspire reading round a subject for background information Adaptable

2. *Meet emotional needs*	Acceptance Belonging Mutual respect Sense of personal value relationships Participation leading to growth self-awareness Awareness of others' thoughts and feelings

3. *Give opportunities for sharing faith*	Natural relaxed atmosphere Conversational approach Sharing of views, listening

4. *Are a springboard for action*	Group not an end in itself Changed attitudes, actions Mutual support in Christian activity Joint ventures in caring

Wall charts are large pieces of paper on which words or diagrams are displayed. They may be prepared in advance or compiled during the session. Alternatively words already on the chart can be covered until required.

Shelf-lining paper or the back of wallpaper can be used. Sometimes large rolls of slightly damaged paper can be acquired from printers. Failing all else, large sheets of paper can be purchased at stationers.

Thick felt tip markers are easy to write or draw with. Separate pieces of paper can be attached to the chart with drawing pins or reusable adhesive.

The advantages of wall charts are:

- they are a visible reminder of what has been said.
- if they are built up gradually during a session they can help group members to understand.
- when completed they serve as a summary which can be copied and kept for future reference.

Flip charts are large sheets of paper fastened at the top. Each sheet is flipped over when it is finished with.

Whiteboards are used like blackboards. Coloured felt markers show up well, and the waterbased ones can easily be wiped off with a damp cloth. Avoid permanent markers unless a permanent record is wanted.

Some whiteboards are magnetic, and sheets of paper can be attached with magnets either to cover details which are not needed or to add words or diagrams to the existing visual aid.

Overhead projectors (OHP) are expensive and the course can be run without one, but if there is one available the trainer will find it useful.

The advantages of the OHP are:

- it is simple to operate
- it does not require blackout
- it allows the trainer to face the trainees while using it
- normal sized writing is used
- one transparency can be placed on top of another to add to the diagram

The disadvantages are:

- there is limited room on one transparency and only one image can be viewed at a time
- the OHP image on wall or screen demands attention, and the user needs to remember to switch it off when it is not required. The constant switching on and off can be disstracting.

To use the OHP, plug in and place in a position where it does not block the trainees' view. Project on to either (*a*) a plain wall, which saves space but the picture may be distorted, or (*b*) a screen. If the projector head is below the level of the screen incline the top of the screen forward to give a true picture.

Transparencies can be single sheet or roll. They are available from stationers. When preparing a transparency in advance rest it on white paper so that you can see the image. When writing on it while in use, the light shining through will enable you to see the image which is simultaneously being projected on to the wall behind you. Do not use the outside edges of the transparency. A few practices will soon bring proficiency and confidence.

Marker pens are available from stationers. They can be waterbased or permanent. The water based ones can smudge if you rest your hand on them; if you need a drawing on the transparency in advance, draw it underneath so that you do not smudge it while adding to it in the session. Remember that the image will be reversed if you draw underneath the transparency. Use bold colours for greater effect.

It is useful to mask out part of the image with a sheet of paper on top and reveal only the parts you need at the time.

The aim of group exercises in each of the sessions is to enable trainees to experience and/or put into practice and reinforce what they have learned so far.

Exercises 1 and 2 are useful in any newly-formed group.

There is no need to use all these exercises; simply select the ones with which you feel most comfortable.

Exercise 1 Early memories

Aim: To enable trainees to get to know each other and by experiencing what it is like to be listened to and feel valued, to have their emotional needs met. To promote a sense of group identity.

Method: The trainer describes some personal early memory of Sunday School or church. Trainees are invited briefly to do the same, either in open session, or in twos and threes.

The trainer next tells the whole group in three or four sentences what is personally important in his or her life. The trainees are invited to do the same, again, either in open session or in smaller groups.

The exercise should last about fifteen minutes.

Exercise 2 Four questions

Aim: As in exercise 1.

Method:
   (i) The trainer describes the house which was home when aged about seven.
  (ii) The trainer tells the whole group about a favourite toy or game recalled from childhood.
         The trainees do the same, in small groups.
 (iii) The trainer describes to the whole group the 'place of warmth' in childhood; this may be a room at home, a corner of the garden, a person, or anything which brought a sense of security and warmth.
         The trainees do the same, in small groups.
  (vi) The trainer describes the first conscious awareness of God in a personal way; this may be from childhood, adolescence or adulthood, depending on the trainer's experience.
         The trainees do the same, in small groups.

Comment: The four questions become increasingly personal, starting with objective descriptions, moving on to the more emotional ones and finally to the spiritual. Most people can move easily from one stage to the next and find that they can talk naturally about their experience of God after they have shared with each other on the other subjects.

Exercise 3 Drawings

Aim: To demonstrate how educational needs are best met through communication which is more than one way.

Method: Trainees are provided with a piece of paper and pencil. The trainer draws on paper a diagram the trainees cannot see and at the same time describes it to the trainees. From the instructions given by the trainer, each trainee does his or her own drawing. Nothing can be repeated, and no questions can be asked. The communication is one way, and is taken at whatever speed the trainer selects. The trainees cannot slow down the flow of instructions. The diagram may

Session One
Presentation

14 consist of circles, squares and triangles. Technical terms may be used (isosceles triangle, concentric circles), points of the compass (e.g. take the line in a northeasterly direction) or anything else which gives an accurate description of what the trainer is drawing. When the diagram is finished the trainer shows it to the trainees and asks to see any which are at all like it. Not many will be much like it!

Repeat the exercises, varying the diagram, but allowing questions, clarification, slowing down, or explanation as required by the trainees. This time the communication should be more effective, and more of the trainees' diagrams should resemble that of the trainer!

Exercise 4 Making a model

Aim: As Exercise 3.

Method: Work in pairs, sitting or standing back to back each with a small table.

Number 1 has model on the table, made from e.g. ten or twelve pieces of lego.

Number 2 has identical pieces of lego on the table. Number 2 cannot of course see number 1's model.

Number 1 gives instructions to number 2 on how to assemble the model. No questions are allowed.

After a specified time, compare models.

Repeat the exercise, using a different model, this time allowing questions.

Alternatively, instead of everyone doing the exercise, ask for two volunteers who can do it while the others observe.

Duration of session one: 50–120 minutes, depending on how many exercises were used.

SESSION TWO

What Makes a Group Function Well or Badly?

Preparatory reading for the trainer

In any gathering of people there is a group process or group dynamic. It is the inter-action between members, caused by the forces that are at work at any one time. Some of the forces are positive and help the group to function well. Some are negative and cause the group to function badly. The group climate is how it feels to the members of the group.

The leader's role is:

1. To encourage the things which tend to make the group function well.

2. To discourage the ones which tend to make it function badly. There are some things which happen within a group over which the leader has little or no control, but there are many areas in which the leader can help create a group climate in which growth can take place.

3. To try to ensure that all needs within the group are met.

1. *Some of the forces at work in groups which tend to make a group function well*

Group members' feelings The group members need to be feeling relaxed, comfortable, accepted, secure enough to take risks within the group and to test out their ideas. They need to feel able to share something of themselves.

Openness and honesty The group members need to be open and honest with each other even in the face of conflict.

Expectations of each other Their expectations of each other and of the leader need to be realistic, not too high and not too low.

Non-verbal communication Being able to see each other is very important as some messages are passed without words. An encouraging smile, a nod of approval, laughter in the right place all help to make the group function well.

Suitable size The group needs to be small enough for everyone to know each other and large enough for members not to feel that too much is expected of them. Ten to twelve members is a good number.

If a group has to be bigger and cannot form two separate groups make sure that you split for part of the time in each meeting, to give the closeness the small group offers.

Achievement There has to be some achievement for the group to feel successful. This may be a thorough investigation of the subject under discussion, it may be the completion of the set number of verses or chapter in the Bible, it may be reaching a decision about what action to take, or it may be compiling and signing a letter to a prisoner of conscience.

Good leadership Styles of leadership and qualities of a good leader are covered in session three. It is sufficient here to say that the good leader will be aware of the forces at work in the group and will actively encourage whatever is helpful.

2. *Some of the forces at work in groups which tend to make a group function badly*

The converse of the points in (1) are applicable here. Some additional points can be made:

Group members' feelings Bad feelings can be nervousness, inadequacy, fears both real and imagined, hostility to the leader or to another member of the group, awe of the leader. Some of these can be overcome by the person who is feeling them, and some will pass as the group becomes established; but if they persist they can be destructive.

Group members' misconceptions (*a*) Misconceptions about the other members of the group. The others are more learned, more capable, more intelligent, more likeable, more acceptable, more everything that is good, than we are! We all feel this sometimes and it arises partly from our own sense of inadequacy which perceives others as inevitably better. It damages the group. All members need a realistic evaluation of themselves and of the other members, with the grace to accept their own and each other's strengths and weaknesses.

(*b*) Misconceptions about learning. There are several misconceptions about learning:
it is passive, and all we need to do is to soak up knowledge;
it should always be initiated by experts; we cannot learn from each other;
it is deadly serious and cannot be fun;
it is all to do with the mental processes and has nothing to do with experience or emotion;
it should be an individual and private matter, and should not be shared in any way.
If group members have any of these misconceptions about learning the group will suffer.

Hidden agendas These will not be immediately apparent but will emerge as the meeting progresses. They are whatever a group member brings to the meeting which will divert the group from doing its job. This may be someone's hobby horse which is always brought up whatever anyone else is talking about. It may be someone's ready-made answers which will be produced and adhered to however much evidence is produced to contradict them, or however many new facts emerge. It may be a member's deep concern about a personal matter. It may be the need to support or oppose the leader at all costs. Any of these can be destructive to group harmony or effectiveness.

Defence mechanisms These may arise out of group members' feelings. When we feel threatened in any way we all tend to use defence mechanisms to protect ourselves. We may revert to childish behaviour such as exhibitionism or sulking if we do not get our own way. We may vehemently deny that something is true because we do not like the implications of it. We may transfer to some kind of scapegoat feelings of anger which we feel are unacceptable. For instance, we do not feel we should be angry with some member of the church so we transfer our anger to the committee system, or the size of the church building. If several people in a group are using defence mechanisms the real work of the group is hindered.

Lack of motivation, aim and achievement Adults, like children, need motivation if they are to learn. Adult motivation often comes from within, but sometimes needs a bit of encouragement from outside. This can be provided by the group having a clear aim, a direction, a purpose, which makes the members want to be part of it. If there is no aim, there is no motivation. The aims can be long term, such as growth in understanding of the Christian gospel, or deeper experience of prayer, or redressing some of the social injustices in the world. The aims can be short term when they are often referred to as objectives. These can be understanding the parable of the sower, or deciding how best to talk to children about God, or writing a letter on a particular point to an MP.

Without aims and motivation, a group will not thrive.

There needs to be some sense of achievement because without it despair can set in.

Non-verbal communication Yawns, snatched glances at watches, sniggers, all tend to destroy a group. Knowing looks intercepted by someone not in the know create feelings of uncertainty and the sense of being excluded. These prevent a group from functioning well.

Bad leadership A bad leader will ignore the forces which militate against good group functioning. Lack of adequate preparation by the leader can be a further cause of bad functioning in a group. If simple questions are left unanswered, if necessary equipment is missing, if subjects are dealt with superficially because the leader has given insufficient time, thought and prayer to it, the group will tend to fall apart. Lack of preparation indicates a lack of respect for the group as a whole and for the individual members.

3. *Needs within the group which the leader should try to meet*

There are three areas of need in a group of which leaders should be aware. They should try to hold the three in balance as far as possible and ensure that all are met at least in part.

The needs of the individual Every member of the group has personal needs. All need to feel that they belong and are accepted. All need to feel that their value is enhanced by belonging to the group. All need to have intellectual stimulation at an appropriate level, not too deep so that they feel out of their depth, and not so shallow that they are not satisfied.

Good group leaders will try to ensure that the needs of each individual are met.

Jesus demonstrated this after Peter's denial, when he restored Peter's self respect by enabling him three times to declare his love for his Lord, and three times commissioning him to feed his sheep (John 21).

The needs of the group as a group The group needs to establish and maintain a sense of group identity, and not see itself just as a collection of individuals. It needs to engage in effective teamwork and to have open and clear lines of communication. It takes some time for these things to happen, and few groups at their first meeting will achieve it, but the needs are there. Good group leaders will try to ensure that these needs are recognized and met.

Jesus took time to explain things to his small band of disciples, giving them a strong sense of group identity (e.g. Luke 8: the explanation of the parable of the sower).

The task needs The task is to work through the subject under discussion, or to complete the activity. Good group leaders will ensure that an appropriate task is set, that it is introduced properly, the main points recognized and discussed, and appropriate action taken.

Jesus sent the disciples out on missions, giving them an appropriate task, while standing by to help where necessary (Luke 9, Matt. 17).

These three areas of need are sometimes in conflict with each other. For instance, one *individual* may come to a meeting with a need to talk about his marriage problems. He may feel the need to talk to one other person there, and not to the group.

The *group* needs to function as a group and does not do this if separate conversations are taking place.

18   The *task* has already been decided upon and needs to be done.

So what do group leaders do? Either:

  (i) meet the needs of the individual by letting him have his private conversation. But that leaves the needs of the group and of the task unmet; or

 (ii) carry on with the planned meeting, satisfying the needs of the task and the group. But that leaves the needs of the individual unmet; *or*

(iii) change the planned meeting, the task, from whatever it was, to a discussion on marriage. This keeps the group intact and meets its needs. It meets the needs of the task in a reasonably acceptable way. In part it meets the needs of the individual; or

(iv) spend part of the time on the task, and leave part of the time for private conversation. This partially meets the needs of the task, the group and the individual. No one of the three has the needs fully met.

The leader's role is to keep a balance between the three areas of need. Good leaders will try to do this in each meeting, but will rarely if ever succeed fully in all three areas. They will try to do it over a period of time so that each of the three areas of need is met at some point within that period.

If too many areas of need are unfulfilled the group will fall apart.

The leader's role is to create as large an area of overlap as possible between three areas of need.

A group which is functioning reasonably well, with all needs being met in part, will look like this.

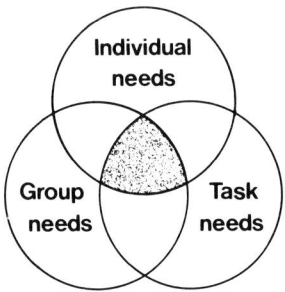

If there are small groups in heaven, they will probably look like this!

Summary

1. Our own experiences in groups
2. Explanation of group forces
3. Buzz groups and charts on group forces
4. Handout on 'Things that can stop a group from functioning well'
5. Three areas of need
6. Handout on 'How to ruin a meeting'
7. Group exercises

1. *Our own good and bad experiences in groups*

Refer to the 'complete the sentences' exercise in session one. Read out a few examples of each of the two sets of sentences from the wall chart you compiled in session one.

If the exercise was not used in session one, ask trainees to formulate one-sentence statements about the best and the worst group meetings they have been in. Hear several or all of these, noting similarities or variety.

Comment that this session is about how a group functions well or badly, and our own experiences will help us to identify what can happen in a group.

2. *The group process or dynamic, the group climate, and the forces at work in a group*

Explain what these are, using the preparatory reading for the trainer on pages 15f.

Ask for two or three examples of good forces and bad forces, from the 'Complete the sentences' exercise.

3. *Buzz groups and charts on group forces*

Start to compile a chart of the things which make a group function well.

After you have written down a few suggestions on the chart, ask the trainees in buzz groups* to think of as many as they can in three minutes.

After three minutes add their ideas to the chart.

> **Buzz groups** are short discussions between two or three people. They deal with one subject for a short time. Members are not put into groups, but simply turn to the people nearest to them. Buzz groups get people thinking and talking about a subject without wasting time. Quieter members, who would not readily comment in the full group, are enabled to state their opinions in the buzz group. If a large discussion group becomes sluggish, or is finding difficulty in getting going, a three-minute buzz can bring it to life.

4. *Handout on 'Things that can stop a group from functioning well'*

See page 21 for handout.

Work through the list on the handout and encourage trainees to make notes under each heading.

5. *The three areas of need in a group*

Explain the three areas of need using visual aids as follows:

Using OHP

(i) *Prepare* three transparencies
Each will have a circle as in diagrams on page 18
In one write 'individual needs', in one write 'group needs' and in the third write 'task needs'. Use a different colour for each.

(ii) *Show* these one at a time and talk about each area of need in turn. Ask trainees for specific examples of needs in each area.

(iii) *Overlap* the circles to demonstrate how the needs of all three may be partially met at the same time. Illustrate this using the example of the person who came to the meeting needing to talk to another person about marriage problems (see page 17).

(iv) *Move* the circles to demonstrate the different ways of handling the situation, with some needs left unmet. Use other illustrations and examples to demonstrate how needs are sometimes met and sometimes not. Move the circles around to demonstrate this. The situations could be:

a group member who needs constant reassurance from the group and keeps interrupting the meeting to get it.

a group which is divided into two or more conflicting camps and cannot see itself as a group.

a task which is too big to be completed in the available time.

a task which is not fully understood by the members.

(v) Once the trainees have understood what the circles represent, and how they can be moved about to illustrate different situations, divide them into buzz groups and ask each group to think of a situation and be prepared to come up to the front to demonstrate it on the OHP.

(vi) *Show* the circles completely on top of each other (concentric) and explain that this demonstrates a situation in which all needs are fully met. Ask how often the trainees think this happens!

Using wall charts or flip charts or whiteboard. The difference in the presentation if you use wall charts instead of OHP is that you will need a lot of paper instead of three transparencies! Use the same method as with OHP except that you will need to draw each circle each time you refer to it. If you use a flip chart, you can stand in the same spot to lead this session. If you have a lot of wall charts all around the room you will need to keep moving around.

At the buzz group stage, give your trainees sheets of paper on which to draw their overlapping circles to show to the whole group.

6. *Handout on 'How to ruin a meeting in twenty-six easy lessons'*

See page 22.

Session Two Humour is a valuable teaching aid, so make the most of this handout. Read it through with the
Presentation trainees, and ask for additional points from their experience.

Things that can stop a group from functioning well

Group members' feelings

Group members' misconceptions

Hidden agendas

Defence mechanisms

Lack of aim and motivation

Non-verbal communication

Bad leadership

Other

How to ruin a meeting in twenty-six easy lessons

1   Put the chairs in straight lines facing the front.

2.   Have the room either too hot or too cold, or ideally too hot at the beginning and too cold at the end.

3.   Have inadequate light and place visual aids where at least half the group cannot see them.

4.   Either assume that everyone knows a great deal and expect a great deal from them or assume that no one knows anything and treat them as if stupid.

5.   Let vocal members dominate always.

6.   Never listen to what anyone else says, but just wait until you can get your next speech in.

7.   Occasionally pounce on a quiet person with a difficult question.

8.   Express horror if someone says something you do not agree with.

9.   Allow members to put each other down with derogatory remarks, and set an example by doing the same yourself where possible.

10.   Suppress immediately any suggestion of genuine personal feelings being expressed.

11.   Encourage platitudes and clichés.

12.   Suppress any suggestions that any action should be taken arising out of the discussion.

13.   Let as many as want to come to the group, preferably more than fifteen as this avoids close contact between members and enables you to adopt the role of teacher. Avoid any suggestions of breaking into smaller groups for discussion.

14.   Do not let yourself think about what is happening in the group but just bat on regardless.

15.   Start late and let the meeting drag on after everyone wants to stop.

16.   Keep looking at your watch and occasionally yawning. Always speak in a bored voice.

17.   Do not allow participation from any but the most boring of group members. Do all the readings yourself and always introduce, dominate and summarize every discussion.

18.   Never permit members to address each other in the meeting. Channel any observations through you.

19.   Never have any variety in presentation of meetings.

20.   Allow and even encourage members to take sides and take up entrenched positions on any subject.

21.   Ensure that nothing is ever satisfactorily completed.

22.   Frown on any sign of humour.

23.   Criticize in a loud voice the behaviour of any children present.

24.   Ensure that the seating is as uncomfortable as possible.

25.   Ensure that there is a telephone in the room and always engage in a long conversation when it rings.

26.   Ensure that there are the maximum number of external distractions.

Exercise 1 The wrecking group

Aim: To demonstrate some of the forces which can wreck a group.

Method: Ask for five or six volunteers to be members of a discussion group to be observed by the others. This is known as 'fishbowl'. The observers have a specific role to play in observing what is going on, but they take no part in it. They may comment later.

Give to each of your volunteers a role described on a piece of paper which no one else must see. (For fuller explanation of role play see pages 34, 53f.).

Suggested roles: 'I'm nervous.' 'I feel inadequate.' 'I am the leader.' 'I should have been the leader.' 'I'm always right.' 'I'm deaf.' 'I always agree with the leader.'

Give the group a subject and ask them to discuss it for 10 minutes each adopting the role they have been given. Subjects should be simple and easy to understand. For instance, 'The use of guitars in church services', 'The behaviour of young people on buses', 'The price of food'.

When the discussion ends, see how many people can correctly identify the various roles. Discuss which was most disruptive, and why. Consider how the leader handled the group, pointing out that it was a very difficult one. Conclude by mentioning any good thing that happened in the group.

Exercise 2 Advice to a group leader

Aim: To enable trainees to think through a situation and work out how best to handle it.

Method: Outline the following situation, or have it written up for all to read on a wall chart or OHP.

Barbara arrives at the housegroup full of excitement about a Christian Celebration meeting she has been to the previous night in which she saw a liturgical dance group interpreting a psalm and a parable. She is very enthusiastic about it and wants to explore the possibility of starting a dance group in the church the group members all go to. She is very eager to talk about it with the group as she feels that some of the members could help her to form a dance group.

Peter, the leader of the housegroup, has planned a Bible study in a series on Philippians and he has already briefed three people to read sections and do a role play.

In *buzz groups* discuss how Peter (*a*) could and (*b*) should respond. After 6 or 7 minutes, ask each group to offer the solution which they feel is the best.

Duration of session two: 100–120 minutes.

SESSION THREE
Styles of Leadership and Qualities of a Leader

Preparatory reading for the trainer

1. *Styles of leadership*

Leadership styles vary from the autocratic dominating dictator type through to the *laissez-faire* spectator, sit-back-and-see-what-happens type. Somewhere in between is the enabler, or facilitator, sometimes known as the democratic type of leader.

In most small group situations the last style is the most appropriate. It is the style we see Jesus using with his disciples, who is the personification of the statement that a good leader can enrich a situation without overshadowing it.

The dictator The dictator type of leader would like to sit out at the front behind a desk, imparting information to people sitting in straight rows in front.

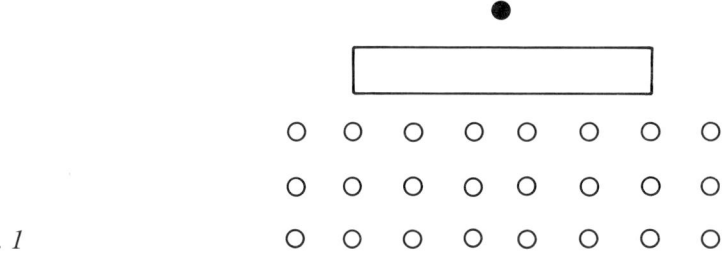

Fig. 1

Leaders of this type may decide to put the chairs in a circle but they will still see their role as the boss, with all knowledge originating from them.

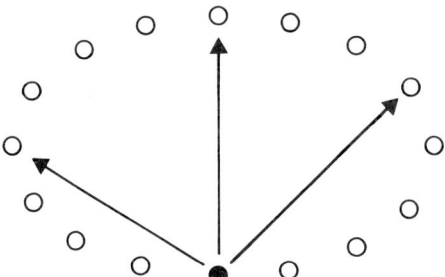

Fig. 2

They are likely to be more interested in the subject matter than the people and will make all decisions themselves. If they ask for the opinions of group members they will expect the members to agree with the leader. They may allow discussion but will ensure that all remarks are addressed to the leader who will answer all qestions and comment on all observations by group members. The picture may well look like this.

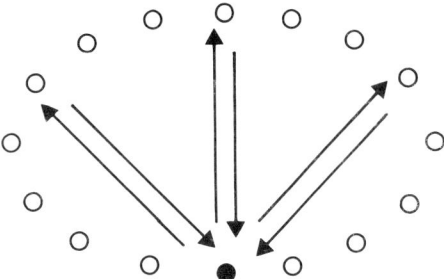

Fig. 3

They will not notice the frustrations, hostility and aggression which develop. Or the group may like this kind of leadership, which makes no demands on them and gives them a sense of security.

This style of leadership may be a sign of the leader's own insecurity. There is a fear of letting go of the reins even for a moment, in case control of the discussion is lost. It takes courage for this kind of person to let the discussion go wherever it will for a while. This authoritarian kind of leader has an emotional need to dominate. An authoritarian leader is not to be confused with an authoritative leader, who is not a dictator but is a person making proper use of authority.

The spectator Leaders of the spectator type will launch the discussion and then let it range where it will. They appear to take no further interest in it. The result is a lack of direction, no firm conclusions and no recommended action. Other members of the group may take on the role of leader and salvage something from the meeting, and this may even have been the aim of the spectator leader who wanted to enable others to share in the leadership. The style can lead to feelings of insecurity and uncertaintly about what is expected from members. They are not made to feel accepted and valued unless they are fortunate enough to be able to do that for each other.

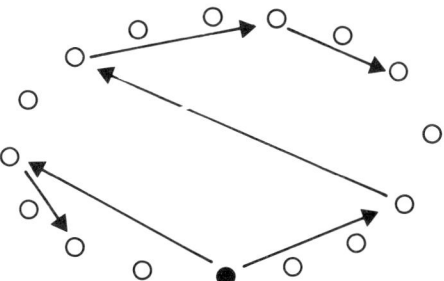

Fig. 4

The enabler Leaders of the enabler type will initiate discussion but will encourage members to talk to each other. Such leaders may be silent for long periods but will be ready to join in if necessary, to seek clarification or draw someone into the discussion who is obviously eager to speak. Every so often the enabler will summarize the discussion so far and at the end will ensure that people know what is expected of them. In general, if other people can be enabled to make points, offer examples or suggest forms of action, the leader will be satisfied. The enabler or democratic type of leader is the one who seeks to maximize other people's freedom and responsibility, not forcing ideas or decisions on to group members. Jesus used this approach in all

Session Three
Preparation

his dealings with people. He gave them a choice and even when their decision saddened him, as in the case of the rich young ruler (Matt. 19) he let them make their own decision. He would always ensure that the true situation was placed before them, and he offered plenty of teaching, but the response to it was their own.

The enabler's major aim is to create a learning situation, a climate in which members can learn and experience things for themselves. The leadership role will be shared with other members of the group. All the resources of the group will be used and there will be sensitivity to the feelings of each member.

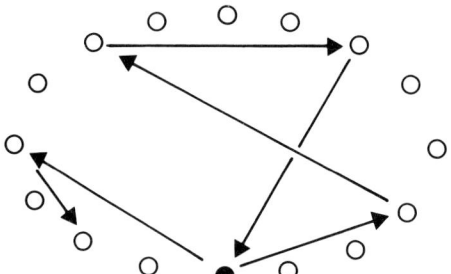

Fig. 5

2. *Qualities of a leader*

A good leader will have some, but not all the following – and will not expect to be the perfect leader!

- a love of the Lord, a desire to grow, a willingness to be exposed to painful situations.
- A concern for other people's Christian growth.
- An ability to listen.
- Sensitivity to others.
- Adaptability to new and challenging situations.
- Willingness to share something of himself.
- Ability to build up good relationships.
- Warmth of personality.
- Sense of humour.
- Willingness to serve and be available.
- Ability to suffer and rejoice with group members.
- Ability to confront members when necessary and to challenge them.
- Willingness to have personal beliefs and actions challenged.
- Ability to accept criticism and absorb hostility without resentment.
- Willingness to put self in a new learning situation from time to time, to experience what it is like to do something new.
- Self-awareness and self-acceptance. Without this he will not be able to be aware of others' inner needs nor will be able to accept other group members as they are.
- The knowledge that whatever value there is in the group, it is God's work in which it is a privilege to share.
- Willingness to share the leadership either in order to receive help or to give training and experience to a potential leader.
- Ability to be present in a situation and enrich it without overshadowing it.
  Willingness to give time to praying and planning and caring for group members.

Session Three
Preparation

Summary

1. Illustrated description of three styles of leadership
2. Buzz groups and wall chart and handout on qualities of a good leader
3. Group exercises

1. *Illustrated description of three styles of leadership*

In advance

If using *OHP* (useful because transparencies can be superimposed on each other) prepare three transparencies:

– one headed 'Styles of Leadership' (this will remain on the projector as a heading for everything you are saying. On the other transparencies leave the top area blank so that this heading shows through)
– one as Fig.1 on page 24.
– one with a circle made up of small circles. Fill in one of the small circles to represent the leader.

The others each represent a group member. This transparency is the basis for Figs 2–5 (pages 24–26).

Have available three blank transparencies, and felt pens.

If using *wall charts* prepare five charts, one for each of Figs 1–5. It is best to add the lines and arrows while you are talking to the trainees as they will more easily understand what the lines represent.

Make a large heading, 'Styles of Leadership'.

In the session

Explain that there are different styles of leadership. We each need to identify our own style and decide whether it needs modifying.

The dictator Put the main heading on OHP (or chart), 'Styles of leadership'. Use Fig. 1 to describe the dictator – behind desk, distant, authoritarian figure. Remove Fig.1.

Create Fig.2. On OHP put the circle transparency. Put a blank transparency on top and draw in the lines to make Fig. 2. On wall chart draw in lines and arrows.

Point out that there is no significant difference between Figs 1 and 2 apart from the seating arrangements.

Create Fig.3 by adding a set of lines parallel to the first, with arrows pointing to the leader.
Point out that here the leader is answering all the questions and fielding all the comments.

Write *dictator* at the bottom of the visual aid and summarize the style of leadership.

Remove the top transparency from OHP, leaving the circle ready for the next Fig.

The spectator Create Fig.4. On OHP put blank transparency and draw on it lines with arrows showing direction of remarks. Start at the leader but do not return to the leader.

On a new chart draw in lines and arrows.

Point out that the leader initiates the discussion but takes no further part in it.

Write *spectator* at the bottom of the visual aid and summarize the style of leadership.

Remove top transparency from OHP.

The enabler Create Fig.5. On OHP put blank transparency and draw lines and arrows starting at leader and occasionally returning to the leader. On a new wall chart draw in lines and arrows.

Point out that the leader initiates the discussion, but allows members to talk to each other, and not only to the leader. The enabler-leader will make comments or answer questions when necessary but is likely to pass questions back to the group for their answers and comments.

Write *enabler* at the bottom of the visual aid and summarize the style of leadership.

2. Buzz groups

Ask trainees in *buzz groups* to describe someone they consider to be a good leader. In the groups list the qualities quickly on a sheet of paper. Let each buzz group in turn make one contribution to a chart until all their ideas have been exhausted.

Add to it from your own ideas.

Handout a prepared sheet of qualities of a leader, either copying the list on page 26 or preparing your own. The trainees may add the group findings to the end of the handout.

Discuss whether any of the suggested qualities is incompatible with others, and in what situations particular qualities are especially useful.

3. Group exercises

Exercise 1 What would you say?

Aim: To give trainees intensive practice in responding to a situation in a discussion group which they are leading.

Method: Set up a small group discussion with volunteers. Appoint one as leader and select a subject. It may be the use of visual aids in worship, the place of women in industry, the difficulty of parking a car in the local car park, or any other preferably topical subject or one of local interest. After initiating the discussion, the leader is told that whenever he wants to speak again he should raise his hand. He does not speak, but other members of the group (or the observers) say what they would have said at this point, if they had been leading. Finally the leader says what he would have said – if he can still remember! This goes on for five or six minutes, with as many or as few interruptions as the leader determines. It can be repeated with other leaders.

After each discussion has been ended, consider the contributions suggested and see if there are any discernible dictators, or enablers, or spectators amongst those who have led.

Exercise 2 Questionnaire: (handout page 29).

Aim: To enable trainees to identify their own leadership styles.

Method: Ask each trainee to fill in the questionnaire on his own but in the same room as the others. This will take about five minutes. This is private and they do not need to show it to anyone else, but they may like to discuss it with someone they trust to check whether they have a correct perception of themselves. Briefly explain the significance of having most As in column 1, which represents authoritarian leadership (the dictator); in column 2, which represents democratic leadership (the enabler) and column 3, which represents permissive leadership (the spectator).

Ask every trainee to think and pray about whether any change is needed in their style.

Exercise 3 Monologue

Aim: A bit of fun. Also to learn, by identifying mistakes, how a meeting should be opened.

Method: Read the monologue on p. 30 and ask trainees to pick out as many mistakes as they can spot.

Discuss the mistakes.

Session Three
Presentation   Duration of session three: 120–130 minutes.

Questionnaire to identify my style of leadership
(Adapted from a Scripture Union questionnaire)

In each column, circle A if this is you, and C if it is definitely not you. Otherwise circle B. At the bottom of each column write in the number of As.

Column 1	Column 2	Column 3
I decide what the group is aiming at A–B–C	I accept that others in the group can be involved in decision making and leadership. A–B–C	I let the group decide the aims and make the decisions A–B–C
I am more interested in the subject matter than the people. A–B–C	I make efforts to create a sense of security and belonging. A–B–C	It doesn't matter what they talk about so long as they are happy. A–B–C
I plan carefully and only feel secure when I control the discussion. A–B–C	I encourage others to speak, and to speak to each other in the group. A–B–C	I prepare little and prefer to see where the discussion goes. A–B–C
I stand slightly apart from the group because I am the leader. A–B–C	I ask for clarification or move the discussion on when necessary. A–B–C	I do not try to regulate the course of the discussion, or evaluate it. A–B–C
I always ensure that the group gets through the material prepared. A–B–C	I try to ensure that the group as a whole is satisfied when the goals are achieved. A–B–C	I say little and give little guidance A–B–C
Total As	*Total As*	*Total As*

Circle the column in which you have most As.

Column 1 represents authoritarian leadership (the dictator) – tight control of group, everything passing through leader. Can result in discontent and frustration within the group. Can provide a safe place for the shy.

Column 2 represents democratic leadership (the enabler, facilitator). Tends to lead to satisfaction and mutual acceptance within the group. Can lead to group pressure on newcomers to conform.

Column 3 represents *laissez-faire*, permissive leadership (the spectator). Can lead to feelings of insecurity and uncertainty about what is expected.

Try to find someone you trust and discuss with them your style of leadership, and whether it is appropriate for your group.

Monologue: 'How not to open a meeting'

Overact without becoming entirely ridiculous. Speak either to an imaginary group, or else use other people present as the group.

(*Walking in, shivering*) Ooh, it's very cold in here. I forgot to switch the heat on.

There don't seem to be many of you here. Better pull close together to keep warm. Where is everyone? This is too bad. Mind you, I did forget to put the notice in on Sunday and last time we weren't too sure when we would meet again, so I suppose the others don't know we are here tonight. They won't have gone to Jane's will they? We did talk about having it there, but I don't think we decided really. There used to be so many people who came, didn't there? I can't think why they all stopped. While we're waiting to see if they come, did you hear that Mrs Fawcett has left her husband? Yes, and he's stuck with all those kids. I really can't think how he'll manage. He used to come to this group, but he'll never make it now. John said he was coming, and it's only ten minutes late, so we'll wait a bit. Oh, good here he is now.

Malcolm, will you open with prayer? No? Well, never mind then, we'll just get going.

What's the passage for today? I can't remember where we got to last time. Are you sure I'm to be leading anyway? Did any of you think you were leading tonight? No? Oh well, never mind, we'll muddle through like we always do. Mind you, I think it's pretty silly studying this book like this. I can't think whose idea it was. No one seems to want to do it. It's so boring.

Hello, who are you? Well, never mind, find a chair and sit down and we'll talk to you later.

Now I think this is the bit. Andrew, can you read say from verse one of chapter four to the end? No, that's a bit long, read about ten verses. It looks a very long chapter. Can't you see over there in that dark corner? Oh, you haven't got a Bible? OK someone else can read it then. Dorothy. Oh, you haven't got a Bible either. Has anyone brought a Bible? No? You didn't realize this is what we were doing? I'll read it then, but this is an old translation – I couldn't find my new one as I was rushing out. My teeth are chattering so much with the cold I can scarcely speak! Anyway we'll struggle on and see how it goes. I don't want to be late tonight because there's a programme I want to watch at half past nine.

SESSION FOUR
How to Set up a Group

Preparatory reading for the trainer

Before your trainees can become leaders of small groups, the groups must be established, and the trainee will need to do preparatory work to bring this about.

1. *Identify the need*

Do people in the church, or in the neighbourhood if an outreach meeting is planned, want to meet in a small group to discuss and share thoughts and feelings about the Christian faith? It is vital before setting up such a group to discover what the potential members feel to be their needs, as they are unlikely to turn up at something they do not want!

Informal chat will soon reveal which people are keen, which are marginally interested and which are totally opposed to the idea.

From those who are interested find out whether they would see the group as a Bible-based discussion, a focus for considering matters of topical interest, a series on the basics of the Christian faith, or something else. By suggesting different possibilities you can widen their horizons and make them aware of needs they were not previously conscious of in themselves. For instance, it may not occur to them that it would be helpful to read and discuss the meaning and relevance of the Easter story from one of the Gospels, but once they begin to think about it, they may realize that that is just what they need to clarify their thinking about the death and resurrection of Jesus.

2. *Be prepared to be like mustard seed*

Do not be discouraged if only a handful are really keen. It is good to start with a small number if you all have the same purpose.

As you become more confident and find that the group is a help to you, you can invite others to join you and build up the numbers gradually. Ten to twelve is the optimum membership. If you launch your group with a great fanfare of trumpets and people attend in vast numbers soon to discover it is not quite what they expected there will be a depressing sense of failure as numbers decline.

Start small, like a mustard seed, and expect to grow.

3. *Consult the minister or priest and the church leaders*

When you have several names and a few ideas of what you might do in a group, consult your minister and anyone else in authority. They may be enthusiastic about groups in the church, or they may have some reservations based on previous experience. When people meet in small groups and enthuse about their experiences there, they can give the impression that they feel that in some way they are better Christians or more spiritual than those who do not meet in this way. This can be divisive and hurtful and its repercussions in a church can last for several years. The minister may want to talk to you about this.

Another concern expressed by the leadership of the church may be that the group could develop along unhealthy lines; members may become too introspective, constantly as it were taking their spiritual temperatures and not making any progress; they may become unbalanced theologically, emphasizing one truth to the detriment of another to the point of heresy; it may be that for the members, the group is beginning to supervise the programme and the content of the meetings or may appoint someone else to do that. If so, see this as a safeguard for you and your group, and not in any way as a threat.

The church leaders will probably have several helpful ideas and may offer more names of people who will be interested. Keep leaders informed of your activities and enlist their help where possible.

4. *Have clear aims*

Decide what the group is for and keep reminding yourself of it. You need both *long term* and *short term* aims. Let group members know what they are: *Long term* aims may be:
    helping new Christians to understand the basics of the Christian faith;
    encouraging Christians to think through the implications of their faith and put it into practice in daily living;
    understanding and responding to the needs of the Third World;
    challenging people with the claims of Jesus Christ;
    Short term aims or objectives may be:
    applying the teaching of Jesus in the parable of the sower to our church this year;
    understanding why the Holy Spirit came at Pentecost and what this can mean for us;
    considering the right use of Sunday for Christians in non-Christian society;
    thinking about the rights of the unborn child and how to preserve them;
    finding out about the work of Traidcraft and planning how to help.

Be prepared to look critically at the group from time to time to see to what extent it is fulfilling its aims.

5. *Select time and place*

Choose a suitable day of the week and time of day, bearing in mind the commitments of the people who want to come. Try to make sure your meeting time does not clash with other groups in the church which cater for the people you are hoping to attract.

Choose a venue which is convenient for as many people as possible. For instance, if someone finds it difficult to travel because of infirmity or baby sitting problems, consider meeting at that person's house.

6. *Plan the first meetings*

When people are wondering whether to come to the meetings they will need to know what to expect. There is no point in offering vague generalizations because that will tend to make people feel insecure and therefore unwilling to commit themselves. Be prepared to be specific and try to sound confident about what you have planned even if you do not feel it!

It is useful to start with a short series of meetings which people can commit themselves to attending. After the first short series they can decide whether they want to continue in the group or not without either feeling trapped into staying or guilty about leaving.

Lent can be a good time to hold a series as people are inclined to feel that they ought to do something for Lent. (There are several Lent books which are ideal for this purpose, with discussion material provided. See Appendix.) But don't wait for Lent if you can conveniently start sooner.

Follow up the first short series with another one until you are reasonably sure that sufficient members want a permanent commitment.

The Bible is the most valuable resource book, but keep looking for useful articles in newspapers, magazines, books, tapes, videos etc.

See session six for different types of groups for different situations.

7. *Publicize the meetings*

Most of us find it easier to go into a group which is starting, where all the members are new at once, rather than join an established group. It is vital to make sure that your publicity reaches everyone who might be interested, in time for them to think about it, find out more, and make arrangements to be there. So publicity needs to be organized in good time. Prepare posters, magazine articles, pulpit notices, typed handouts giving the date, time, place and purpose of the meetings, and make it clear who it is for. A specific invitation to a limited group will get a better response than a very general invitation which causes everyone to think it is meant for someone else!

For instance, if it is a group for older teens and early twenties, put something like this:

Are you between 17 and 23? Do you want to understand more about the Christian faith? Then come along to . . . etc.

Decide on the target for your publicity, and aim straight at it.

All publicity needs to be backed up by personal invitation, and nothing is more effective than 'Come with me to. . . '

8. *Prepare the room*

Prepare the room and be ready in good time for the first meeting so that you are free to welcome people as they arrive and introduce them to each other if necessary. Make sure the room is warm enough and that people will be comfortable. A cup of tea or coffee at the beginning of the first meeting is a useful ice-breaker. After about twenty minutes of informal chat, giving people the opportunity to get to know each other a little, start the meeting fairly positively so that those who are pressed for time will not feel that they are wasting it.

Presentation of the session

Summary

1. Brainstorm and chart
2. Handout on 'How to set up a group'
3. Group exercises

1. _Brainstorming_

Invite trainees to call out as quickly as possible all the things they think they might need to be done in order to set up a new group. This is called a brainstorming session in which any ideas are acceptable, however unlikely they may seem.

Write the ideas at random on a chart. Make it a big one, so that the trainees know there are lots of things to say! When ideas stop coming, draw out more by asking leading questions.

2. _Handout on 'How to set up a group'_

Hand out sheets of paper listing the headings from the preparatory reading on how to set up a group and ask trainees to put under each heading the relevant points from the chart. Have an additional space at the bottom for ideas which do not fit any of the eight headings. (Page 36 contains a sample handout which can be photocopied.)

Allow a few minutes for this to be done. It can be an individual exercise or completed in twos.

Ask for any additional ideas which have occurred to trainees.

There will be discussion about several points. Try to save this until the handout sheets are completed, and deal with the points section by section. Not everyone will agree about everything, but that does not matter provided they have had an opportunity to think out what is most helpful in their own situation. Something which would be excellent in one church could be just the wrong thing for another.

3. _Group Exercises_

Exercise 1 Role play

Aim: To clarify thinking on how to set up a group and to enter into a different way of looking at things.

Note on role play: Role play involves setting up a situation in which people take on a character or a role and act out an impromptu sketch in which each person plays out his own role and reacts with others. It has many uses, one of which is to enable individuals to enter into other people's attitudes and more easily understand other people's actions.

Some trainees may find it difficult to play out a role that isn't their natural one. They will need encouragement.

Others may overact through silliness or embarrassment. This doesn't matter provided they do not prevent others from entering into and using their roles.

Method: Divide into pairs. One of each pair believes that all you need to do in order to set up a housegroup is to pray and people will come. The other believes that you need to plan. Give each one a minute or two to think about the role, and then ask them to hold a conversation, each sticking firmly to the role allocated. The main purpose will have been achieved by now, but it may be fun to listen to one or two of the conversations if trainees are willing to repeat them for the whole group.

Exercise 2 Write a letter

Aim: To reinforce what has been learned about planning a group.

Method: In small groups prepare a letter to the church council explaining what you are proposing to do, and how you intend to set about it.

Put the finished letters on a notice board for others to read, or read them out as if at the church council.

Duration of session four: 60–90 minutes.

How to set up a group

1. Identify the need

2. Be prepared to be like a mustard seed.

3. Consult the minister and church leaders

4. Have clear aims

5. Select time and place

6. Plan the first meetings

7. Publicize the meetings

8. Prepare the room

SESSION FIVE
Subject Matter for Different Types of Group

Preparatory reading for the trainer

This session is about what to do in a group meeting. Session six is about how to do it.

There are innumerable different situations each calling for a different type of group meeting. This section lists some specific types of group with a selection of things to do in each. Clearly, many of the ideas can be used anywhere, while others are useful only in selected groups. The Bible is our handbook and guide and all groups would be well advised to make use of it in some way: some will build most of their meetings around it, and discussion will arise from it; others will use it as part of a series on a subject using a variety of sources; others will have an epilogue after an activity based meeting. In all groups, the Bible needs to have a place.

The types of group listed here are representative rather than exhaustive. Groups 1–8 are described by this constituent members, groups 9–11 by their function.

1. The multi-purpose, all-age group
2. Those exploring the faith
3. New Christians
4. Young people
5. Young mums with toddlers in tow
6. Men
7. Young couples
8. Mature Christians
9. Prayer groups
10. Bible studies
11. Worship groups including dance, drama, mime and music

An alternative way of describing groups is according to their subject matter. There would be, for instance, the Pilgrim's Progress group, the Mark's Gospel group, the Family Relationships group. After a while they would change their subjects and there would be, for instance, the Letter to the Roman's group, the Issues Facing Christians group, etc. People are able easily to join or re-group when a new subject is taken up.

Another way of describing a church group for publicity purposes is according to when they meet – the Wednesday nighters, the Sunday at eight group, etc.

1. Subject matter for the multi-purpose, all-age, group

The average church is likely to have one fellowship group catering for all comers. The diversity of experience will be enriching to all in the group and will see it through many years of useful life. The danger is that the group can get into a rut and always do the same kind of thing in the same way, because it has worked well before. The leader may give a short talk which is followed by discussion; a topical subject from the newspaper may be introduced followed by a general airing of views on the rights and wrongs in the situation; or group members may always read a passage of the Bible and answer questions about it. Whatever it is, if it is always the same the vitality of the group can be lost taking with it the likelihood of personal growth.

Variety is stimulating, both in type of subject matter and presentation. Here are some suggestions to lend variety:

Visual aids are useful in several ways:
(i) they can *introduce a subject*
– eg The Riding Lights video by Lella in which any of the ten short sketches can introduce a discussion eg on miracles, how to care for people, about gossip;
– or the 'Visions' video produced by Rob Frost of the Methodist Church, with nine Biblical incidents depicting the work of the Holy Spirit;
– or, much less expensive than videos and soundstrips, use pictures or posters to introduce a subject, such as water, or the bread of life, or light. Pictures from magazines can be used to good effect, or make your own visual aid, either a collage made from printed pictures and words, or write or draw what you want, and develop it during the meeting to focus attention and aid understanding.

(ii) they can *illustrate a point*, eg in a Bible study on James' letter, faith in action can be illustrated by a snip from the 'Jesus Then and Now' series of videos, number five on lifestyle, with Jean Vanier and his community for mentally handicapped and normal people.

Or you can build up a chart to illustrate how the cross is the bridge between sinful man and a holy God. What people see they are more likely to remember. See Appendix for further details.

1. At first the picture shows that man is separated from God by sin.

2. Adding the cross of Jesus to the pictures shows how the gulf is bridged.

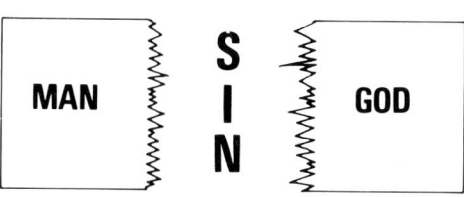

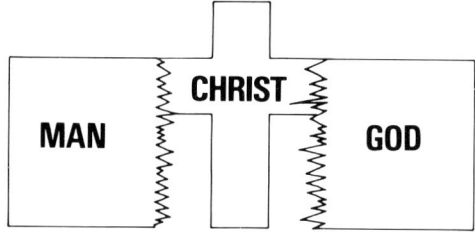

(iii) visual aids can be the *main part of the meeting* and be left to speak for themselves. There are many films and videos and soundstrips on the market, most of which can be hired from local Christian bookshops or from a central office. See Appendix.

Sharing the leadership is stimulating and brings variety. Preparing the meeting together can be beneficial for the leaders who can bounce ideas off each other and become more adventurous than some would be on their own. It takes more time to prepare together but it is worth it for the leaders and for the group. Taking it in turns to lead lends variety, and although some will be more experienced and comfortable with it than others, the group will accept the less experienced leaders if most of them are prepared to take their turn. It is surprising how less critical we are when we

Session Five
Preparation

know we are going to do the job ourselves sometime! If one person always leads others will be very diffident about taking over when need arises. From time to time invite the minister or priest to answer or comment on some of the accumulated questions.

Sharing a meal is fun, it makes a change and gives opportunity for informal conversation. It's a chance to get to know people in a different way, and subsequent discussions are enriched because you know more about each other as people.

Working together on a project draws people together and can reveal hidden talent. Someone who has sat in silence through meetings may come to life when a person is needed to organize a stall selling Traidcraft produce at the local market. Those who are less articulate will be delighted to demonstrate their faith by taking part in a sponsored fast or Christian Aid walk. Visiting a local children's home or refuge for battered wives and working out ways of helping are good activities for all-age groups.

Planning a service focuses attention remarkably and can bind a group closely together. It will increase their understanding of their chosen or allotted theme and will make them more aware of the ingredients of worship as they put the service together.

Following the main Christian festivals can give a sense of purpose and progress throughout the year. There may be discussion about Christmas customs throughout the world, a Bible study on the meaning of the incarnation, a filmstrip telling the Christmas story, and a visit to another church's carol service or special Christmas service. Lent may give opportunity to visit other churches and Easter could feature a prayer vigil and a Good Friday meditation, with a Bible study or a series of studies on the Easter story. Pentecost could include a visit to a charismatic group or service, a discussion about the Holy Spirit in our lives, or an analysis of some of the Pentecost hymns. An ambitious group could put on a musical presentation for the rest of the church! Harvest could involve helping with decorating the church, giving out harvest gifts to the elderly and the sick, with a commitment as a group to keep on visiting the housebound where appropriate.

The group could undertake a harvest project to help the Third World in some way. Then it is on to Advent again. . . In Methodist churches the annual covenant service merits study in a group and if this can be done before covenant Sunday, the service can be so much more meaningful.

Celebrating holy communion as a group from time to time, with the minister or priest presiding, is a possibility.

2. *Subject matter for those exploring faith*

Around any church community there are people who wonder what it's all about, what makes Christians tick, where God fits in, who Jesus is. They may be a bit cynical or suspect that the church is a club where people find refuge from the harsh realities of life, but they would like to *know*.

Some of them will dare to 'come to church'. It's a big step for them to enter into an environment and a culture which is unknown to them, and they show great courage if they make it to one of our services. Hopefully, they will be made welcome, and not pounced on immediately to become a Sunday School teacher, Youth Leader, or whatever the current gaping hole is in the running of the church. As well as being made welcome they will need to have someone to talk to, somewhere to ask questions without feeling either ignorant or unacceptable. They need to explore the Christian faith if they are to be able to decide whether they want to be part of it or not.

A housegroup or small group in a church coffee lounge offers the ideal opportunity (see session one for the value of small groups as an opportunity for sharing faith). If the minister or priest and the church members are alert to opportunities they will be able to find the people who would appreciate a group to explore the Christian faith and its implications. They could be parents who have their babies baptized and would like to learn more about the church into which their baby is being welcomed; couples preparing for marriage; parents of Sunday School children; people who

Session Five
Preparation

use the church premises for other activities; those who have been helped through a personal tragedy by the minister or a church member.

We cannot force our faith on to people and we must be sensitive to their feelings, but we can make sure that they know that it is on offer and that they can explore it without any commitment.

A five week course run two or three times a year can be publicized on notice boards, through pulpit notices and church organizations. If all church members are aware of when the next course starts they can invite any of their friends or contacts, perhaps offering to go along with them. It is the initial step of inviting them that is hard, and we all tend to hesitate before doing it. A quiet enquiry along the lines of, 'We're having a series of meetings for people who want to find out more about the Christian faith. Do you think you would be interested?' cannot cause offence and could produce a positive response.

The group could be for one church if there are enough interested at one time, or for a circuit or part of a circuit. A local group of churches where there is co-operation between denominations could do it jointly.

The contents of the course will depend on the needs of the people who come, and the questions they are asking. At the opening session the leader can ask for a list of questions they would like to ask and the programme for the rest of the meeting can be built on these. There will probably be one meeting devoted to the meaning of God, and one to who Jesus is. Here are seven possible approaches:

– *Word game* A well-tried method of talking about Jesus is to ask members to call out a word they associate with the name of Jesus, and put all their words on a wall chart. This may involve childhood recollections, or current experience, or something they have read. When the flow of words dries up look at them all, discuss them, finding out whether people agree with the associations, and what they mean by their words, and so on, giving opportunity for further questions to be asked. The leader's comments will act as a catalyst sparking off further thoughts, and leading the group in helpful directions. A clear and convincing picture of Jesus will emerge and members will begin to feel that they know him, or at least that he is worth knowing. Some groups will get into discussion about Jesus being God and/or man, others will want to talk about his healing powers, others about his teaching. Try to ensure that as many aspects of the teaching and ministry of Jesus are touched upon, and come back another time to any really big issues which catch people's attention.

– *Lifestyle* A session on lifestyle can be challenging as much to Christians as to those exploring the faith. Thinking about what we consider to be Christian standards in a non-Christian world. Some Third World information and some details about poverty in our own country will ensure that the discussion is firmly based on reality. The 'Jesus Then and Now' video previously mentioned is a thirty-minute programme on lifestyle which will provide plenty of food for thought. Discuss in particular what we feel we should do about our standard of living, if anything, and in what ways our attitudes need to change.

– *The church* A session on what the church is and what it is for may give rise to the expression of a number of old or new grievances. The same word game could be used here as on the subject of Jesus. Make it clear that the church people do not think they are any better than others, but that the church is a body of forgiven sinners, meeting to worship God and to serve the community.

– *Panel* A few people invited in to answer questions about how their faith works out in practice will remove some misconceptions the enquirers may have. A living example of a Christian who is enjoying being one, in spite of the struggles, will have real impact on those who are still uncertain.

– *Good News Down the Street*, a Grove booklet, offers a programme of study for a group such as this, with a practical, effective and realistic method of setting it up.

   The course could be used as a pre-membership one from which hopefully some of the group members would go on to membership training.

– *Third World Issues* can be a challenge to Christians and non-Christians alike, when we are confronted with not just the vested interests of large companies, but with our own personal vested interests and innate selfishness. An honest look at some of these issues can lead to an awareness of sin, the need for forgiveness, and a new life in Christ, the Transformer of our attitudes.

– *Homework* in the form of private Bible study gives opportunity for quiet reflection and questions which can be brought to the next meeting. Many people find faith while reading or praying at home, having received teaching and encouragement from the group.

3. *Subject matter for new Christians*

As with those exploring the Christian faith, new Christians need to have:
1. Opportunities to ask questions and not be ridiculed for them.
2. Encouragement to pray regularly and systematically, perhaps using a notebook; to read the Bible perhaps using one of the many daily Bible reading aids (see Appendix);
   to share their beliefs and doubts with other Christians and to share their good and bad experiences:
   to learn to talk to new friends about their new-found faith in a natural and acceptable way.
3. Help in sorting out their priorities in time, abilities and money with discussion about areas of their lives in which they are beginning to feel uncomfortable since becoming Christians.

Ideas for basic Christian teaching
- A course of Bible study on Mark's Gospel.
- Selections from the gospels introducing Jesus and the people he met.
- A series on the letter to the Ephesians in six sessions.
- A series on the meaning of the cross, the resurrection and the ascension.
- Discussion on how and how not to witness to others.

Ideas for application of Christian faith
- Discuss attitudes to war, work, racism, ambition, money, sex, violence, etc.
- Give each person or small group a newspaper and ask them to pick out a few items and give a Christian comment on them. Share thoughts on this.
- Think about the local community and try to identify some of the needs. Decide what as a group or as individuals you can do and *go and do it*!
- Find out about some aspect of local politics and take appropriate action – lobby members of local council, attend meetings, write letters or whatever you can to bring about what you believe is right in that situation.

Suitable materials

– 'Growing more like Jesus' (CPAS) is a nurture group course for new Christians and contains ideas for Bible studies, with worksheets which can be photocopied, and worship ideas.
– 'Beginnings: Conversation starters' and 'Beginnings: Big questions' by Rob Frost, (Bible Society) are Bible-based discussion material.
– See Appendix for more materials.

Session Five
Preparation

A small group of serious-minded young people from twelve or thirteen upwards will make great strides in the Christian faith given appropriate teaching, encouragement, and space to think and feel and sort things out for themselves. There are many books available with ideas. A few are mentioned here. Others are in the Appendix.

In general young people appreciate variety within a framework. For instance, the framework could be a theme such as peace; a series of meetings on the theme could be presented in a variety of ways, including a speaker, a debate, a Bible study, a filmstrip, a discussion, some drama, and could lead to some specific action promoting peace (writing letters, joining a march or a lobby). Finally a service could be prepared on the theme to be offered on a suitable Sunday in the following quarter.

Some activities will be *quiet and thoughtful*, such as discussions, Bible studies, planning for action. Others will be more *action-packed* and may take place out of the usual meeting room. All discussion should lead to something, often a change of attitude or a decision to take some action about behaviour. Useful way of ensuring that discussion is not just an intellectual exercise is to have a 'lifestyle activity' by asking what change the discussion requires of each individual and suggesting that each selects one small thing in his life and commits himself to take some action on it.

The *action-packed* activities can be purely social, which gives opportunity for members to get to know one another better and also to bring their less committed friends. Barbecues, visits to roller rinks and skating rinks, ten-pin bowling alleys and local concerts all help to bind a group together. Young people's natural desire to be together can be channelled into useful and practical activity – though they should never feel that they are unpaid servants of the church, doing all the practical jobs that no one else has time for! They can help with gardening, shopping, decorating (with care!) visiting the elderly and the housebound. They may be prepared to make this a regular commitment and they will gain a great deal from the experience of sharing in a conversation with the elderly.

They might join a lobby for the unemployed, or write jointly to their MP stating how they would like him to vote on an issue about to come up in Parliament. They might organize and take part in a Hunger Lunch in aid of the Third World, or have a sponsored fast. Ambitious groups can undertake an all night sponsored disco in aid of an organization like the National Children's Home.

All these activities can be seen as the outworking of their Christian faith, and the fun is infectious.

Music is a significant part of youth activity and it can be a great deal more than simply strumming a guitar and singing choruses. They may like to write their own songs and use them in a service at church. Percussion instruments are cheap and can be used to great effect as an accompaniment to bring a joyful tone into singing in church. They can develop the art of using background music for Bible readings, or after a discussion to give time for meditation on what has been said. Music used in conjunction with appropriate slides as a background to a reading can be very worshipful. Young people like modern music, and if they are not able to produce their own – or even if they are – they can arrange a visit to a local Christian rock concert, or plan to invite a group to their own church. This can be a useful form of outreach and a small group of young people can do great things here.

Outreach. Young people are particularly good at bringing their friends to whatever they are interested in, and that includes church and group meetings. Squashed together in someone's sitting room they will feel at ease and will happily share ideas about what matters in life. The input of an audio cassette such as the Disciple cassettes with the Riding Lights Theatre Company and Garth Hewitt, with a commercial radio sound and a well-presented Christian challenge, will go down well. Rock On cassettes explore the rock message on various topics. They can listen to some of the current top twenty and discuss the morals, the attitudes and the expectations they give rise to. If young people are encouraged to look in to the Bible for themselves the gospel will speak for itself, and young Christians will begin to help each other in understanding what God is saying to them as they discuss the Bible together.

Session Five
Preparation

Worthwhile meetings do take place amongst the prams and the toys and the potties, and young mums are often more than delighted to have the opportunity to talk about something other than feeding times, nappies and playgroups. A crèche can be organized if the children are too distracting, with mums taking it in turns to look after the children. Anything at all can be discussed about the Christian faith and Christian living and there is a wealth of material available to help the leader. Bible study outlines, discussion outlines, books on topics, apart from all the audio visual resources.

Here are three suggestions for programmes covering several meetings.

The role of women can be explored by looking at
- women in power (politics, business, education etc)
- women in the church
- women and health and beauty
- women and sex
- women in the Bible
- A study on Mary the mother of Jesus can round off the series.

Food for thought and thought for food can be developed with reference to parables about food, our attitude to what we eat, healthy eating, mealtimes and what they are for, eating while others starve.

Bringing up children can include questions such as how do I discipline my children? Can children be kind? Children's fears, children's questions, children and church. See especially Margaret Sharp, *What Do We Really Want for Our Children?* (Epworth Press 1986).

6. *Subject matter for men and for single people*

It is difficult to get men to meetings, and in some areas the best way to do it is to limit the group to men and to involve them all in the planning. They will talk in the pub and at the club, but seem reluctant to talk at church, or to meet in each other's homes. A small group of men meeting for a meal followed by a speaker with discussion afterwards is more likely to attract them than a formal gathering in a room at church.

A series of big topics such as economics and the Christian, unemployment and Christian values, the Christian in politics, marriage and the family, health and stress, the Christian at work, Third World economy, pacifism, may draw the men in. If each takes it in turn to introduce a subject and to chair a meeting, they will feel committed to the group and will be more likely to attend.

Categorizing people on a sex or family basis is not always helpful and single people can easily be left out. They should always be catered for when groups are formed in a church and the 'big topics' listed above are likely to interest them.

7. *Subject matter for young couples*

Couples in their twenties and early thirties were fairly recently the young people, and they will still be interested in some of the same things. Because they get married and have children they do not become entirely different! Ideas from section four will therefore be useful.

New interests will be homemaking, bringing up children, career, the problem of making ends meet financially, and relationships within the wider family of in-laws. These should appear in any programme of meetings for a small group. A useful series on relationships could include marriage, children, people at work, neighbours, extended family, caring for elderly relatives. Each could be Bible-based and could include helpful sharing of experiences. The Bible Society has two useful booklets of Bible study sessions, 'Challenging Relationships' and 'Family Relationships'.

Session Five
Preparation

Garth Hewitt's music and style is popular with this age group and his six songs about the church called 'The Bride' based on the letter to the Ephesians make excellent Bible study and discussion material. 'The Bride' is in the form of a soundstrip (SU) including the songs. It is helpful to write up the words of the songs before the meetings, or else provide each person with a copy of the words as there is so much in them that people cannot remember what they have heard.

Several other songs can be played and discussed from a Christian angle, whether they are overtly Christian ones or not. The Beatles songs have made a come-back in recent years and provoke a great deal of thought and comment.

Occasional family days when the families share in a picnic or an outing will help to bind the couples together in their shared joys and problems and will help the children to feel that they are part of the family of the church. Family camping weekends are fun and can build up relationships.

If the group can plan and lead or take part in a service in which their children can join, they will develop a greater sense of belonging together to the church.

8. *Subject matter for mature Christians who want to deepen their faith*

It may be that in your church people who have been Christians for many years feel the need of others of like mind to stimulate and challenge them. It is likely that these mature Christians will be helping in other groups too, but they will feel the need to come together for a meatier diet to satisfy their own needs. Leadership here is likely to rotate, though one person may naturally fit the role to everyone's satisfaction. There is likely to be in-depth Bible study, working systematically through a book of the Bible, with several members reading the commentaries and preparing for the meeting.

Each meeting will probably offer time for prayer and reflection, and the emphasis will be on learning from the Holy Spirit and from each other's understanding and experience. A useful exercise is a study week by week of significant theological words. William Barclay's *New Testament Words* (SCM Press 1964) provides some source material for this, together with a concordance. There is the danger of this becoming purely an intellectual exercise, and it is important to remember that any new insight should have some effect on us. A discussion of the meaning of grace is incomplete without some thought being given to the areas of our lives in which we have received, or just now need, grace. An understanding of justification should lead to the response of gratitude to God for what he has done. Each year several Lent books are published. A group of this kind could undertake to read one and share their thoughts at the end of each week.

From time to time members may want to discuss something topical, and to work out together the Christian angle or angles on it.

In the Methodist church the various Divisions produce reports and the group could undertake to study each as it comes out, with a view to submitting their findings and thoughts where appropriate. Recent ones have been Marriage and the Family, In Search of Health and Wholeness, Church Membership and Christian Nurture, and Sharing in God's Mission, in addition to the annual Home Mission Report. The Church of England produce reports and the recently produced *Faith in the City* (Church House Publishing 1985) will provide hours of study! (An abridged edition is available.) So too will *The Nature of Christian Belief* (Church House Publishing 1986).

9. *Subject matter for prayer groups*

Session Five
Preparation

Some groups meet with the primary aim of praying. Prayer may be introduced by a devotional reading with comment. There may be a hymn sung, or a psalm said together, or someone may spontaneously lead in the singing of a familiar chorus. There will be a time for praising God in whatever way is appropriate – with words, music, perhaps movement and silence. There will be time for confession, in which it may be helpful to think quietly over the last week and ask forgiveness. From time to time a member may need to confess aloud something which is a burden, and be assured by the leader of the forgiveness of God to those who truly repent.

There may be a time of sharing of personal needs leading into prayer for each other. The group can sit in silence while each prays for the person at his left; members can pray aloud for each other one by one, with everyone concentrating on one person at a time and offering them and their felt and unknown needs to God: each in turn may sit in the centre and all the group lay hands on them and pray silently. However it is done, the praying for each other is strengthening and the power and healing which God offers can be experienced.

Some time will be spent in prayer for others. If this is introduced by conversation great care needs to be taken to avoid gossip. It is better simply to offer a person's name and pray in silence than to break confidences.

There may be list of prayer needs circulated at the meeting, or prayers may be offered as they occur. Some churches have a box in the church porch for prayer requests which provide material for prayer in the group. Others sources for intercessory prayer are the church notices and calendar of events in the coming week, the daily newspaper and missionary magazines, including the missionary prayer manual.

The purpose of the prayer is not to tell God what he should be doing, but to open up the situation to enable him to enter it and transform it however he chooses. Sometimes it will be best just to ask that he will work out his purposes through the situation which may look to us desperate or hopeless.

A church which has a faithful group of people praying regularly for its life and work and witness and for the needs of the world is a church with power.

10. *Subject matter for Bible study groups*

The Bible study and prayer group should be central to the life of the church and should not be seen as additional housegroups for those who have a particular interest in that kind of thing! A church in which a large proportion of the members meet to read and discuss the Bible and its implications is a church which has a dynamic that will bear fruit.

See session six for different methods of studying the Bible.

11. *The worship group including drama, dance, mime and music*

Many churches have groups which plan worship together. Although their main function is the planning of worship, they can also be seen as a small group within the church as much as the Bible study group or the exploring the faith group, and as such they experience the same group processes and have the same needs as individuals and as a group as anyone else. Their task needs (see session two) are specific and will naturally tend to dominate but individual and group needs are there to be met as well. The worship group will have component parts, including such things as music, dance, drama and mime. These may be represented on the worship group by their leaders, or everyone may meet together for part of the time if numbers are small enough.

Part of the time, the component groups will meet separately to do their own thing and that is where a close and mutually supportive fellowship group can be built up. The regular meeting will be a source of strength to the members.

The drama (or dance, or mime) group will take the selected theme and together read and study the relevant Bible passages and any other readings. At this stage the aim is as any other study group – to understand as fully as possible and with everyone participating, the implications of the passage or theme. At some point there will probably be a time of prayer, and a suitable warm-up

46 session before the group gets down to the business of experimenting and exploring different ways of communicating the message. When everyone is reasonably satisfied that as a group they have got to the heart of it and have found suitable ways of presenting the message, the rest of the time will be spent practising, memorizing and perfecting the presentation. This may take weeks. The Resources Appendix lists several books to assist leaders of dance, drama, mime and music groups.

Summary

1. Identify the types of groups and consider suitable subject matter for each
2. Group exercises

Either talk about the different types of groups and some of the things they can do, using ideas from the preparatory reading as well as your own ideas. Encourage trainees to take notes.

Or make a list down the left hand side of a large chart of the different types of group, adding to those suggested in the preparatory reading according to your own ideas. The worship group is omitted from this because of its different nature. On the right hand side put suggestions as to what the groups can do. Use suggestions from the trainees as well as your own.

Group exercise

Aim: to enable trainees to use some of the ideas they have heard in order to plan a series of meetings for particular groups. A bonus is that at the end of it there will be ten prepared programmes for the trainees to take home and use in their churches.

Method: Prepare in advance ten large cards or sheets of A4 paper. Each will have a heading indicating one of the first ten types of group, and a theme for a series of meetings. Choose themes suitable for each group, but avoid ones you have already described in your talk to the trainees about things suitable for different groups.

Space out numbers one to six down the left hand side.

Ask the trainees to work in twos.

Each pair selects a card, looks at the headings, showing type of group and theme, and alongside numbers 1 and 2 writes down ideas for a meeting, being as specific as possible, and bearing in mind that these are two out of six meetings.

After minutes, return the card to the table, and take another card, and do the same. Some pairs will be doing meetings three and four on a card on which another pair has filled in meeting one and two.

After five minutes return the second card to the table and choose a third, and so on until all the cards are completed with a programme of six meetings.

Read out all the cards, and ask for observations.

Put the cards where everyone can see them.

Allow time for details to be taken from them for later use in home church.

Duration of session five: 90–120 minutes.

SESSION SIX
Methods of Group Study

Preparatory reading for the trainer

In session five we looked at the contents of meetings and considered what subject matter was suitable for different situations. In session six we look at methods of group study.

The *group members*, the *content* of the meeting and the *methods* used are like three parts of a jigsaw.

We start with the group of *people*.

We then find subject matter or *content* which is suitable for that particular group of people.

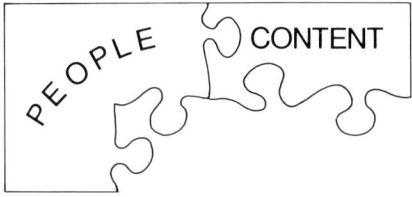

We need to find a *method* which is suitable both for the people and for the subject matter.

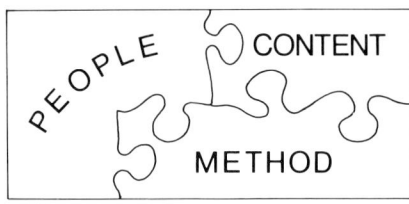

In other words, in selecting a method we need to bear in mind what best suits the purposes of the group; we need to bear in mind the aim of the meeting, the content or subject matter, the ages, abilities and aptitudes of the group members, and the time available.

In order to get the jigsaw together – to have a good meeting – the leader needs to have the group, the content and the method in mind.

There follows a list of methods, or techniques, which can be considered by the leader in making preparations for the meeting. In selecting a method there are two other points to bear in mind.

Some methods may be new, and the leader will need to persevere if they are to be used effectively. He or she may not feel very comfortable with them, but it will be worth persevering if the group can benefit.

The more adventurous leaders may be carried away with some of the methods and be tempted to use them because of their appeal, rather than because of their suitability to the situation. This will not make for a good meeting!

Summary of methods covered

1. Question and answer
2. Visual aids
3. Ice-breakers
4. Buzz groups and slips of paper
5. Questionnaires
6. Discussion
7. Dramatization, mime and dance
8. Interview
9. Role play
10. Dialogue
11. Debate
12. Visiting speaker
13. Case studies
14. Newspaper cuttings
15. Creative writing
16. Analogies
17. Drawings
18. Problem solving
19. Guided meditation
20. Silence
21. Simulation games
22. A Swedish idea

1. Question and answer

Questions are the basic tool of small group work. They are a method in themselves, and are used in conjunction with most of the other methods. Asking the right questions in the right way is not as easy as it appears. There are different kinds of questions which are appropriate in different situations; and there are different ways of asking questions.

Different kinds of questions

Open questions open up the discussion, make people think and lead to general discussion.
e.g. What would you have done in that situation?
Has anyone any ideas about that?
What are your first impressions of that?

Closed questions lead to a limited range of possible answers. They are useful for drawing things to a close, making decisions, or summarizing.
e.g. Do you agree with that?
Shall we write that letter?
Will it be better to leave that until next time?
Questions can be divided in a different way, cutting across the open and closed kinds.

Questions relating to thoughts encourage people to express their thoughts about the matter under discussion.
e.g. What do you think about that? (open)
Do you think that that statement is true? (closed)

Questions relating to feelings encourage people to express their feelings.
e.g. What does anyone feel about that? (open)
How did that picture make you feel? (open)
Did it make you feel sad? (closed)
It is important to formulate the questions carefully in order to elicit answers which will achieve what you want. This is different from putting answers into people's minds – it is more a matter of moving things on in a helpful way. The wrong kind of question can cause the group to dry up.

Session Six
Preparation

As well as open and closed questions, and ones which bring out thoughts and feelings, there are other choices to make in the formulating of questions.

Questions should be neither too difficult nor too easy.

If the question is too difficult, there will be no response because group members will not be confident enough to venture an answer.

If it is too easy they are likely to be too embarrassed to answer, or they may think there is a catch.

So pitch the questions at the right level.

Choice of words is important. They need to be such that group members can understand them at one hearing. Something like 'What is the effect of the juxtaposition of the concepts and faith in this verse?' is not easy to unwrap without a good deal of thought. It is simpler to understand when it is written down, but there is no opportunity to look back over it in a speaking situation. Simple words in short sentences are much more helpful.

Different ways of asking questions

Some people ask questions as if they are firing shots from a gun, or giving schoolchildren a speed test! It is better to deliver the question as if you have only just thought of it (even though you may have spent ages formulating it!) in a pleasant relaxed manner, particularly when you are starting a discussion. Closed questions which are aimed at finalizing decisions can be snappier.

Look at the group members rather than at your notes as you ask the questions.

Be prepared to repeat the question in a slightly different form until you observe a spark of understanding or possible response in someone's eyes.

Acknowledge all answers, otherwise group members feel a bit put down. After all, if you have spent ages screwing up your courage to offer a comment or an answer, it doesn't make you feel good to have it apparently ignored!

If the answer is not what you had in mind, but is another way of looking at the question, or shows a slight misunderstanding of the question, do not declare proudly that that is wrong, but rather say something along the lines of, 'Yes, that's one way of looking at it that I hadn't thought of. But what do you think about. . . ?' and go on to rephrase your question.

If the answer is in your opinion totally wrong, and you feel that the group can handle conflict, then take it head on and disagree. Otherwise ask what other members of the group think. Some members can more easily accept a difference of opinion with another group member than with the leader, and you need to be sensitive to this.

Finally, in the way you ask questions, be gentle and do not rush people into answering. Silence can be productive.

Always know at least one way of answering your own question in case a group member throws it back at you!

2. *Visual aids*

Jesus was a master of visual appeal. He used it in the simplest and most effective way, by pointing as illustration to whatever was already there for all to see. John 4 – the fields white for harvest – may well be speaking of the fields they could all see, or even the white clothes of the villagers as they flocked out to see Jesus at the invitation of the Samaritan woman. In Matthew 8 he speaks about the foxes having holes and the birds having nests, and he possibly pointed to the holes and the nests as he spoke. In Matthew 10 when speaking about the hairs of your head being numbered we can imagine him touching the hair of someone close, or even indicating a rapidly balding head nearby. The inspiration for the parable of the sower may well have come from watching a farmer out there scattering the seed, and the other farming parables arose from what was there for all to see.

There are two kinds of visual aids: expensive and cheap.

Cheap ones are sometimes the most effective. They can be pictures from magazines, or posters or your own drawings or a collage made by the group. They can be bits of stone brought in to illustrate how we are all stones being built up into the living temple in I Peter 2. If group members take the small piece of stone home with them it can serve to remind them that they are part of something special.

They can be a few grapes on a stem to illustrate the vine in John 15.

They can be straggly specimens of plants to illustrate the parable of the sower.

Flash cards (words written on a large card) with headings or main points of the meeting will help to focus attention and aid later recall.

Wall charts have been mentioned and have been found to be very useful by many group leaders.

Expensive visual aids

Overhead projector. Ways of using this are described on page 12.

Audio cassettes. There are many audio cassettes on the market. (See Appendix on resources). All they require is a cassette player and a wall socket where it can be plugged in. (Batteries can be used instead of mains, but replacing them can be expensive.) It is difficult to listen to a cassette for more than a few minutes without something visual to focus on. It helps to have the main points summarized on a handout or chart, or questions to bear in mind while listening. It can become embarrassing constantly to catch someone's eye which tends to happen if there is nowhere to look.

Soundstrips, filmstrips, slides. A soundstrip is a filmstrip with a tape-recorded commentary. Again, there are many available. (See Appendix on resources.) You will require a strip projector, a wall socket, and a screen or a plain wall. The room will need blackout. Most projectors can take filmstrips or slides, having an interchangeable head.

Soundstrips require a cassette player as well.

Videos. This is an increasingly popular and effective way of using visual aids in housegroups. A video machine and a television are required. The advantages are that there is no need for blackout, there is no film to thread through and the medium of television is a familiar one. Many homes are now equipped to show videos.

Visual aids are tools to aid the leader of the small group. They are not an end in themselves and do not do the work for the leader, who still has to plan the meeting, and ensure that group members understand the material and are enabled to get as much as possible out of it.

If visual aids are used without careful planning they can be a distraction rather than a help. If they are meant to introduce discussion, then they should do that, and not simply be a form of entertainment. If they are to illustrate a point, it should be the main point of the meeting. If they are summarizing a series of meetings they should offer a fair summary, not leaving people feeling frustrated because of the inadequacy of it.

3. Ice-breakers

Very useful when a group is formed, to break down barriers of shyness and embarrassment. See page 8.

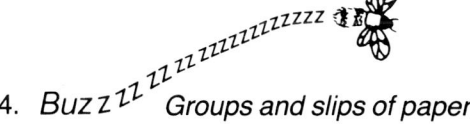

4. Buzz z ᶻᶻ ᶻᶻ ᶻᶻ zzzzzzzzzzzz Groups and slips of paper

Useful when a discussion is not flowing freely.

Slips of paper can be given to each buzz group with a simple unambiguous question. This gives the group members confidence that they have understood the question. Slips of paper can be

Session Six
Preparation

handed out as people arrive, either giving them something to look up in advance and read out at the appropriate point in the meeting, or giving them something to be thinking about and perhaps to discuss until the meeting formally begins. This can give a sense of purpose and save the embarrassing small talk which no one can escape. (Small talk has its advantages, too, in helping some people to relax).

5. *Questionnaires*

Bigger pieces of paper! These can be filled in individually or in small groups. They help group members to think out their response to a situation before they need to speak about it.

Questionnaires can be phrased in such a way that they elicit information which can be used later. E.g. How many times in the last month have you been to church? What do you think is the most important office in the church? What is your favourite hymn? Such information can be collated and conclusions can be drawn from it.

They can enable group members to explore their own attitudes to a situation or an idea. E.g. Does this make you feel angry/happy/frustrated sad? How would you react in the situation described?

Multiple choice questions asking for responses marked (a) (b) or (c) can be collated by the person filling in the questionnaire if guidelines are given for interpreting the answers. These need very careful planning if they are to be accurate. An example is given on page 29, on My Style of Leadership. This kind of questionnaire is popular in magazines, exploring such things as attitudes to sex, responses to real life situations etc, and can be adapted to fit the Christian scene.

6. *Discussion*

Open Open discussion takes place when there is no predetermined outcome. The leader has no preconceived ideas about where the discussion will lead and does not attempt to impose his or her own ideas on the group. The Leader's task is to clarify, summarize and keep the discussion moving at a reasonable speed. He will also seek to draw conclusions at the end, arising out of what has been said.

Structured Structured discussion follows a predetermined course. The leader will achieve this by delivering a series of questions which will move the discussion in the direction he wants. Learning will take place, but group members may feel manipulated. If they feel they have achieved something worthwhile they will be happier about the method.

7. *Dramatization, mime and dance*

Dramatization involves taking an incident and acting it out. A written script is not necessary, and can inhibit the actors. If the incident is long it should be divided into scenes. Discuss the content of each scene, the characters involved and the development of the action. Different groups may explore the various characters, entering into their feelings and discussing their likely responses. Gradually group members begin to feel familiar with the incident and are ready to begin dramatizing it. Within agreed guidelines the actors say what they feel is appropriate, and a drama evolves. When it has been rehearsed several times it becomes reasonably fixed and the actors are increasingly confident about what they are doing. The aim is not to produce a polished performance but to understand the incident and its implications. It is therefore important to discuss the incident again afterwards to summarize any new insights. Small groups will benefit from this exercise. They may not choose to act, but simply to speak, especially if space is limited or if they feel a bit hesitant about moving around. This method can be used effectively with many of the healing incidents in the New Testament, some of the parables, and many incidents from Acts of the Apostles.

Mime is similar in terms of preparation, but the actors do not speak. Someone may read the words as the scene is mimed, or the mime may be used on its own without words. Background music can be helpful. The passage will be studied first and taken apart to discover what it is about, what its main points are and how the people in it would be feeling. Some time can be spent with everyone in the group working out how to mime, for instance, the actions of Blind Bartimaeus.

There is no need to perform the mime, as the very process of working out how to do it will achieve the desired result. Sometimes there will be opportunity to use in a service some of the things which have been worked at in the small group, but that is not to be seen as the aim of the exercise. It may be that out of the small group there will emerge a drama group or a mime group or a dance group (see below) which will begin to meet specifically for preparing to take an active part in worship.

Dance is distinct from mime and dramatization, though again there are similarities. Mime is drama without words. Dance is an expression of something less tangible. Dance is harder for the inexperienced and may need the help of an expert. However, even without an expert, some group members will be able to express joy in movement, or interpret peace in a group, or depect internal strife by wringing hands and holding the head. It must be said that some people will be too inhibited to do this, and no one who does not want to should be trapped into trying. If a whole group will enter into it without selfconsciousness and with enthusiasm it can be a very liberating experience and one which binds the group together.

Dramatization, mime, dance, and the interview method which follows are particularly useful for Bible study groups. See Appendix for resource books.

8. *Interview*

Working in pairs group members can take the part respectively of interviewer and character, and produce an interview which brings out the main points of an incident and offers an interpretation of it. The aim will be to get to grips with what the incident is about and what it means, and the interview is really only a means to that end. In order to formulate the questions the interviewer needs to dig deeply into the story, as does the character in order to give appropriate answers. The interview may be presented to the rest of the group by way of a summary of the story.

As with dramatization, it is vital to have discussion afterwards to spell out what new insights have been gained from the exercise.

9. *Role play*

An extension of interview method, where the character being interviewed took on the role of that character, entered into his thoughts and feelings, and expressed them.

Role play is useful for exploring people's reactions to situations; first the reactions of the people who were actually in the situation; this may be the Bible character, or the enraged parent or the disgruntled employee; secondly the reactions of the group members to the revealed reactions of the people in the situation.

For instance, a group member may take on the role of a person with a grievance against his mother. As the scene is set and the person taking the role of mother has her say, the 'son' may gain great insights into the causes of rebellion and the feelings of injustice experienced by teenagers. This is a valuable exercise in empathy, that is standing in someone else's place and understanding how he or she feels. After the role play, the 'son' may be surprised at how he reacted in the role, and others may be surprised, horrified, pleased or saddened by his reactions.

Role play enables people to *explore reactions of others*, by experiencing them in the role play, and it enables participants and observers to explore their own reactions to other people's reactions. It is clearly vital to have discussion afterwards about what was happening in the role play. It is important to enable the participants to get out of the role, and it needs to be made clear when they are in the role and when out of it.

The other function of role play is to enable participants to practice different ways of responding and reacting to situations. This is especially valuable in dealing with difficult relationships and with tension and conflict. It can be done in one of two ways.

(*a*) If a member of the group has a particular problem with a relationship at work, at home, or at church, he can be himself in the role play, and other people can represent the others involved. This will enable him to explore a difficult situation without risk, and will help him to practice his responses. This method is moving very near to counselling, and needs to be handled with great sensitivity and care.

(*b*) A real or imaginary situation may be depicted, with group members taking on the different roles, and practising responding in that situation. The experience gained will help members to observe the consequences of certain reactions and responses and will give practice in making helpful and appropriate responses, in preparation for real life situations. It will be useful to change roles to see if reactions change. Members should not select a role for themselves because they are likely to select the ones they most naturally play. Growth comes through standing in someone else's shoes. The role play method helps group members more fully to understand themselves and others.

10. *Dialogue*

Similar to interview and similar to role play, but distinct from both.

Working in pairs, group members prepare a conversation each taking a different standpoint on a subject. This is more intellectual than role play or dramatization, and is useful when clear thinking is required.

They may discuss whether the resurrection happened or not, or whether sports teams should go to South Africa, or whether the church council should appoint a full-time youth worker. Each one needs to gather facts and information and think out his angle on the subject. A handout may be provided with relevant facts for each person.

The dialogue can be presented to the rest of the group for discussion.

11. *Debate*

Again topics where there are different points of view can be dealt with, but more formally in a debate, than in dialogue. There will be a proposer and a seconder on each side, and normal rules of debate will apply. The proposer speaks to the motion, which may be 'This house believes that women should take a more prominent part in decision-making in the church' or 'This house believes that all church services should cater for the whole family' or 'This house believes that the human rights issue is the most important issue in the world today' or 'This house believes that evangelism is the most urgent task of the church.' The opposer speaks against the motion, and the seconder in favour of the motion replies to him, after which the seconder against the motion replies.

This formal method of dealing with the subject enables the main point for and against to be presented concisely. After this there will be general discussion, referred to as points being made 'from the floor.'

Session Six
Preparation

At the end of the debate there will be a vote on the motion. On many issues where Christians hold different and equally valid viewpoints it is important to allow both sides to express their views without any feeling of being judged for them; a debate provides this opportunity.

12. *Visiting speaker*

Small groups function best on their own for most of the time, as the presence of a different person, especially someone seen as an expert, such as the minister, changes the group dynamic. However, from time to time it is helpful to call upon the experts, and it stimulates the group if occasionally the group dynamic is changed.

If questions have arisen during the course of a series of meetings which no one else in the group can answer, these can be dealt with in one planned session by someone who does know the answers. If a particularly difficult or specialist subject is being considered, it will be wise to call on the specialists. For instance, if the discussion is about experiments on unborn babies, and the moral implications of that, a local doctor or paediatrician may be called in to give the facts about the beginnings of life in the womb, and the stages of development. If the subject is political prisoners, and how best to help them, a local member of Amnesty International could be invited.

If there is concern about care for the elderly in the neighbourhood a representative from Age Concern will be helpful.

The specialist may provide a very exciting and worthwhile evening, and the temptation may be to repeat the exercise frequently. This is to be avoided if the group wants to retain its character as a small group. If, however, everyone agrees that visiting speakers are preferable as a general rule, the decision must be faced, and the group must change its form and its purpose.

13. *Case studies*

Case studies are descriptions of real or imaginary situations which are discussed and then used to illustrate principles. The principles may be biblical, taken from a particular Bible passage, or they may be more general principles in line with Christian thinking.

The situation is described and discussed. It will have been selected by the leader because it illustrates the principle or principles he wants to explore with the group.

For example he may describe a group of people whose attitudes in a church group leave a lot to be desired; one may be very full of his own importance, one may feel totally inadequate, one may feel that his job is the most important in the group, another may quietly get on with welcoming the others, getting the chairs out or making the tea. The descriptions may be written out on pieces of paper or on one big chart for all to see. The group discusses the various attitudes depicted. There follows a Bible study of Rom. 12. 3–8, and 1 Cor. 12.12–31a, from which several principles will emerge. These will then be related to the case history described at the beginning.

The idea is to make the case study as realistic as possible so that group members can identify with the situation, and then apply the biblical or other principles to real situations which they meet.

14. *Newspaper cuttings*

Cuttings from recent newspapers may be used as material for the case history. Alternatively they may be used simply to introduce a subject such as violence, conflict, anger, greed, selfishness. A selection of newspaper cuttings glued to pieces of card can be passed round and read, to set the scene and give people illustrative material for the discussion which will follow.

15. *Creative writing*

Younger groups enjoy *compiling a newspaper* or just a newspaper article on a given subject. It may be a biblical incident or an up-to-date situation on which there can be Christian comment. It can include imaginary interviews with biblical characters, such as the centurion at the cross, or Amos, or Nehemiah. There can be editorial comment, eye witness accounts, pictures and advertisement. Choice of headlines is thought-provoking and causes people to think deeply about what the incident is really about.

Letters can be written to biblical characters, or to modern world or national figures, commenting on their actions or attitudes from a Christian point of view.

Poems or *prose* may be composed expressing feelings or new insights to be shared with the whole group, or in a service.

Articles for magazines may be prepared in small groups summarizing the group's findings in a series of meetings and making recommendations for action to be taken in the light of what has been discovered.

Some people will have the ideas, others will have the gift of stringing the words together, and others will be useful for bouncing ideas off. Teamwork can produce a useful piece of writing.

16. *Analogies*

Many people find it difficult to express their feelings. Use of analogies may help them.

For instance a group may be asked to express their mood in a *colour*: blue for sad, yellow for happy, black for despair etc. This will help them to clarify as well as express their feelings in terms which other people can understand. They may be asked to find a piece of *music* which most aptly depicts their mood, or the mood of the group or the church. Thinking about *shape* to represent their perception of themselves or some other person can clarify to themselves what they really feel. Similarly they can think of an animal which best describes how they see themselves or each other.

This is only an introduction to something else. The group may go on to discuss God's view of his people, or the difficulties we have in evaluating ourselves realistically, or our misconceptions about other people's view of themselves. A group which does this exercise honestly will find it revealing and liberating, and members will be bound more firmly together through it.

17. *Drawings*

Similar to analogies, but on paper. For instance, a Bible study on the life of Peter the apostle may be depicted in the form of a *graph*, with high spots and low spots. Group members may be asked to draw a graph of their own spiritual pilgrimage in a similar way, and then to share these with each other. A study of Bunyan's *Pilgrim's Progress* could include the compilation of a graph to depict Christian's ups and downs.

On a *scale* 1–10, group members may be asked to mark where they feel they are for instance in their commitment to Jesus Christ.

On a *line* they may be asked to put a cross to show where they are, for instance in their understanding of the Holy Spirit. A more ambitious project is to ask group members to draw and then share with the others a map representing their life so far, with its pitfalls, mountain top experience, calamities and watersheds. Simple *line drawings* of things that we fear or hope for, or to depict what is important in our lives can be revealing, and can give the less articulate group members opportunity to express themselves.

Session Six
Preparation

Adults learn by facing up to and solving problems. This principle can be applied to learning about faith. The idea is to present the group with a realistic problem and set them to solve it.

For instance the problem may be how to explain the Christian idea of forgiveness to a crowd of rowdy teenagers; how to raise sufficient money for a mission in the area; how to prepare people for church membership; how to convince members of the needs of the Third World.

In working together on a realistic solution to the problem, ideas will be clarified and learning will have taken place.

19. *Guided meditation*

We are so used to words and activity we can easily lose sight of the art of meditation. It is a valuable tool for the Christian.

A guided meditation is one in which the leader depicts the scene and leaves silences for the listeners to fill in the details in their imaginations.

It may be a journey back into their own past, with the leader asking them to picture a room where they had a good/bad experience; the people there; the events leading up to the experience; the feelings at the time; then leading back gently to the present and enabling them to reflect on that experience.

It may be a journey into a biblical scene, with the leader talking about the healing of the man brought by his four friends to Jesus, or the visit of Mary to the tomb on Easter morning. The silences will allow the listeners to enter into the thoughts and feelings of the people there, and will give them insights into what happened.

20. *Silence*

We tend to be afraid of silence, because we find it embarrassing or threatening. If well used it can be helpful in a group, as in guided meditation (see above). Silence can be used positively to give group members time to think about a question which has been asked. Or to reflect on what they have learned in the meeting. Or so consider how they should respond in a particular situation. If the leader is comfortable with the silence the group is likely to be happy about it. God speaks to us when we listen, and we often need to stop and listen, as individuals and as a group.

21. *Simulation games*

There are some of these on the market aimed at helping people to understand the problems and pressures of life, especially in the Third World. The Trading Game is perhaps the most well known, about Third World development, produced by Christian Aid. Star Power is a Christian Aid trading game which illustrates power and powerlessness in groups and societies. There is Drug Round about health care and the Third World from the Methodist Church Overseas Division. The games may be played on a board on a table, or on the floor, with people moving around as the game proceeds.

It is possible to devise games which demonstrate certain principles such as the encounter with evil and temptation and the conflict with good, rather along the lines of snakes and ladders.

A useful exercise is to create a game which demonstrates some of the factors which influence our lives. See *Using Simulation Games* and *More Simulation Games* by Baker and Marshall, published by Joint Board of Christian Education of Australia and New Zealand. Also *Simulation*, a handbook for Teachers by Jones published by Kogan Page.

Session Six
Preparation

58   22. *A Swedish idea*

This is a well-known method of doing Bible study. Prepare postcards or sheets of paper as follows:

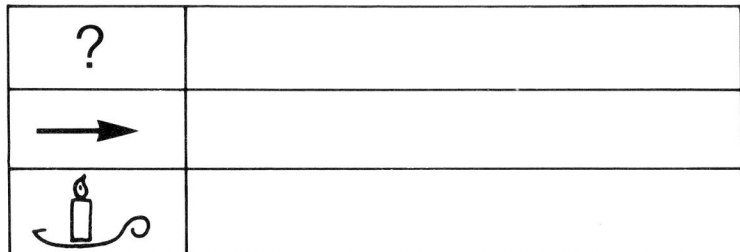

Read the Bible passage. Ask group members in twos or on their own to put at the side of the question mark anything they do not understand.

At the side of the arrow, indicate anything which needs action.

When everyone has completed this, discuss first the points at the side of the qestion mark, then the points at the side of the arrows.

Either in the meeting or later at home, group members fill in by the candle any new insights they have received.

There are many other methods or techniques which can be used to good effect in small groups, and many of the ones listed here can be adapted to suit a particular situation.

Summary

1. Explanation of the three ingredients of a meeting
2. Information about twenty-two methods of group study
3. Discussion on how to ask questions
4. Group exercises

1. *Explanation of the three ingredients*

If using an OHP, prepare one transparency showing the word 'People' and draw a shape round it, using about one-third of the transparency. Prepare a second transparency with the word 'Content' and draw around the word a shape which fits in with the 'People' shape. Prepare a third transparency with the word 'Method' and draw around it a shape which fits in to both the other shapes. If you want to illustrate that some methods do not fit the subject matter or the people, prepare several more transparencies with 'Method ' within shapes which do not fit in to the 'Content' and 'People' shapes.

If using a wall chart, prepare separate pieces of paper for 'Content' 'People and 'Method', cut into shapes which fit together. Misfit shapes with the word 'Method' can be used to illustrate wrong choice of method.

Explain the three ingredients of a meeting, starting with the group members, the 'People'. Show the pictures. Add to it the 'Content', explaining that this is the subject matter which was described in the last session. And that it needs to be suitable for the People. Take the word 'Method' and show that the method selected needs to fit in with the 'Content' and the 'People'.

2. *Information about twenty-two methods*

Prepare twenty-two wall charts, each describing one of the methods in the preparatory reading for the trainer. Place these around the wall.

Prepare a handout listing the twenty-two methods with headings and as much information as you want to offer about each.

Point out the twenty-two wall charts, each describing a different method of group study. Add more if you like. Give out handouts with list of twenty-two methods.

Allow trainees 30–45 minutes to wander around making notes and asking questions about the methods. Be on hand to answer questions.

When trainees have gleaned all the information they want, make any general comments arising out of their questions and observations.

3. *Discussion on how to ask questions*

Photocopy the handout on page 62 and give one to each trainee. Read it through with them, making comments as necessary.

4. Group exercises

Exercise 1 Asking questions

Aim: To demonstrate how not to ask questions, and enable trainees to work out how it should be done.

Method: Hand out to each trainee a slip of paper containing one question. Give them time to think about it and decide how to ask it when his turn comes.

The questions are listed on the next page, and can be photocopied. Add any others to the list.

Take one question at a time. Listen to it. Ask for comments from the trainees on what is wrong with the question, in formulation or the way it was delivered. Discuss that. Ask for comments on how it could be improved. Make sure that the person who delivered the question has opportunity to comment on how it could be improved.

Deal with each of the questions in this way.

Exercise 2 Selecting suitable methods

Aim: To give trainees practice in selecting suitable methods for given situations.

Method: Use the ten prepared programmes which were created in session 5 (see page 47).

Ask the trainees to add suitable methods for each session on each of the ten programmes, working in small groups on one programme at a time.

Alternatively, work out in advance another set of situations, each describing a group and the subject matter and ask the trainees to select suitable methods for each meeting.

Duration of session six: 90–120 minutes.

Questions for group exercise 1 in session six

Doesn't anyone know the answer to this? I would have thought it was quite obvious. I can think of at least three.

What is the ultimate effect of the presentation of the apparently conflicting concepts of life and death in this verse?

That answer is obviously rubbish. Just think about it and you will see how wrong you are.

What does anybody think about abortion?

What was that you said? I wasn't listening. I was looking to see from my notes where we can move on to that would be more useful.

I'm not terribly sure about this, in fact the whole subject completely confuses me and I am quite out of my depth. It would have been better if the minister had led this discussion because I'm no good at leading groups anyway even if I understood what it was about. But anyway here are one or two tentative questions. They're probably all the wrong ones anyway.

That's marvellous! Will you say it again? I never thought anyone would be so clever as to think of that. Amazing!

What did Ananias do? And what did Sapphira say? And why do you think they did that? And what was Peter's reaction to it? And what about all the people watching? Can anyone answer any of these questions?

How to ask questions in group discussion or Bible study

1. Keep notes unobtrusive.

2. Look directly at the members of the group as you speak to them.

3. Relax – and smile.

4. Speak confidently but do not try to give the impression that you know everything about the subject under discussion.

5. Ask questions to which you know at least one answer.

6. Use words that are easy for everyone to understand.

7. Keep questions short and capable of being understood at one hearing.

8. Be specific – vague generalized questions are impossible to answer.

9. Pitch the questions at the right level – neither too easy nor too difficult for the group.

10. Ask questions which make people think.

11. Do not give the impression that there is only one correct answer and that you are waiting for it – there is often more than one possible way of answering a question.

12. If you feel that an answer offered is on entirely the wrong lines, do not say that it is wrong, but suggest that there might be another way of looking at it.

13. Listen to and acknowledge every answer with a suitable response.

14. If silence follows your question:
    Be prepared to ask the question again in a number of different ways until you see a spark of understanding in someone's eye; *or*
    Break the question down into parts and deal with a bit at a time; *or*
    Ask a number of subsidiary questions which will point the way to the answer to your main question.
    Do not appear shocked, whatever answers are given.

SESSION SEVEN
Problems or Opportunities?

Preparatory reading for the trainer

Some of the problems have been considered in session two, 'What makes groups function well or badly'.

As well as the fundamental problems mentioned there, there are several possible occurences which can give trouble to the leader or can be used as opportunities for learning. Warning of these allows the leader to anticipate and plan how to handle them when they arise.

1. *Too talkative member*

One person who is too talkative can ruin a group. He is likely to annoy the other members, and cause them either to see the inwardly, or give up, sit back, taking no further interest in the discussion. The talkative person may not want to talk so much, but having started, may not know how to stop; the longer he goes on, or the more often he does it, the harder it is for him to be any different.

The group leader needs to help him.

A light remark such as, 'Come on, let's give someone else a chance. We've said enough,' will be a broad hint, and will not offend because it is involving the offender in the leadership team, and the leader is as it were standing with him.

A more direct appeal to the other members, such as 'Let's hear what someone else has to say' gives them the opening they may have been looking for, so that they can join in without interruption or appearing rude.

If these gentle methods do not have any effect, and the talkative member persists, to the detriment of the group as a whole, then the leader needs to take stronger action. The leader may have a quiet word after the meeting, asking the talkative one to co-operate by drawing other members into the discussion. It may help to involve him in the preparation of the next meeting and explain to him that leaders should not talk much. The leader may point out that not everyone knows as much/has as much experience/is as confident in a group as 'you and I' are, and others need to be enabled to participate. Enlisting his co-operation is likely to be effective, unless he is very self-centred. Failing all else, the leader will need to tell him that at the next meeting he should only speak when asked to.

2. *The silent group*

Newly-formed groups are usually fairly reticent and are not likely to relax and chat easily until they have to some extent assessed the other members. Ice-breakers or warming-up exercises are a help (see pages 8). If the group is still too quiet to function effectively after several meetings, various measures can be taken.

The first thing is for the leader to get to know the members of the group individually. A good leader will want to do this anyway, as part of the pastoral responsibility of the task, but through knowing and understanding them the leader will be able to draw them into discussion sensitively and appropriately. It is very difficult to go in and lead a group of total strangers, but once you know your members it becomes easier.

On page 71 there is a prepared handout giving seven practical hints on how to get a group talking.

3. *Red herrings*

These may be the hidden agendas referred to in session two. There are two kinds of red herring:

(*a*) The subjects which are brought up by someone trying to be funny or awkward or to demonstrate some specialist knowledge or to shock the leader or other group members.

These should be dealt with in a fairly summary manner, with a remark such as, 'That's not quite what we are talking about today, so we'll leave that until another time.' If the speaker is likely to be offended, and if the subject raised is an interesting one for the group, it could be noted and dealt with fully at a subsequent meeting. If several small subjects of this kind arise over a period of time, a separate meeting can be held to deal with them all at once. This saves producers of red herrings from feeling too frustrated!

(*b*) Subjects which are raised because they are a real problem to a group member. These need more sensitive handling.

If it is an intellectual problem, such as how Jesus can be both God and Son of God, or whether miracles happened in biblical times in the way in which they are described, then it can probably wait until a more convenient time. Again, a special meeting can be set up to deal with it, or an expert can be called in to talk about it. If it is something the group leader can adequately answer, but it is not relevant to the whole group, arrangements can be made to talk to the person in private.

If it is an emotional problem, and is urgent, then a swift decision must be made about whose needs should be met on this occasion. See the three areas of need, session two, with examples and suggestions.

4. *Difficult questions*

Sometimes a group leader is taken unawares by unexpected questions. If an answer does not come readily to mind, the best thing is to admit it honestly, and ask if any one else in the group has any answers. If no one can help, arrange either to find out for next time, or seek expert help.

It is never wise to pretend we know, when we do not. No group leader knows everything – no one knows everything, except God – and it will be good for the group to see that the leader is not someone who has arrived but someone who, like them, is still travelling.

5. *Arguments*

Arguments do arise when people talk together, and sometimes they can become heated.

Disagreement is not bad in itself, and conflict can be creative if handled well. There are many areas in which Christians have genuinely held differing views, and the aim in a group is not to change other people's views, but rather to understand why they think how they do, and enable them to understand our thinking, even if we cannot agree. It may be that some members will change their minds as a result of discussion or even argument, but it is more often the case that people polarize and take up an even more entrenched position when someone disagrees with them.

The function of the leader is to allow everyone to have his or her say; to prevent members from saying things which they will later regret, or in a way which they will regret; to notice and take action when members are becoming unreasonable perhaps because they feel trapped; to clarify what everyone is saying and to summarize the different views at the end. The leader's job is not to pour oil on troubled waters, to ensure that everything appears harmonious when it isn't, because that causes frustration, but rather to enable members to speak the truth in love.

6. *Troublemakers*

Not many people will come to someone else's home to a meeting in order to cause trouble, but it can happen and can be very unpleasant if not handled well.

In young people's groups there are sometimes members who seem intent on being disruptive. (Adults are more subtle about it!) The leader of a young people's group will be well advised to get to know the members particularly well if they are inclined to be a nuisance in meetings. It may be that they are simply needing attention, or that they are testing out their leader's patience. If the leader understands what makes them as they are steps can be taken to gain their co-operation. The teacher's traditional device of giving the naughty child a job to do is a useful one!

Disruptive adults may be needing attention too. They may be needing affirmation of their own value, and when they feel accepted and valued for what they are, they may settle down and co-operate fully in the group. Loud behaviour and brashness often cover a basic insecurity and if this can be dealt with the problem will go away. The same approach may be taken as is taken with the too talkative member; enlist his aid in the leadership and ensure that he understands his role.

7. *Uninterested members*

A survey of why people came to a housegroup once revealed that almost half were there first and foremost for the company. This may be more common than we think. As leaders we are planning what we feel are meetings which are vital to the growth of our members, and it is disconcerting to discover that it doesn't matter to them what we do so long as they can be together!

In a sense this is no problem, but rather an opportunity. They are there, and their needs are being met. Provided they do not distract others who want to learn about specific things there is no harm done. There is always the chance that they will learn something, that their thoughts will be stimulated and their attitudes questioned and perhaps changed.

If the majority of the group are not really interested in what is happening, the group climate will be different and this can cause a problem. The leader will need to work very hard indeed to achieve anything. A solution may be to have one in four meetings for social purposes, and explain that the other meetings are for discussion or study. Additional occasions for being together may be found, such as Saturday walks, or family outings or trips to the theatre or a concert. If group members' social needs are met in other ways they will be more inclined to concentrate on the discussions at the meetings.

8. *Shortage of time*

If a meeting is going well it will probably feel to the members as though it should have gone on longer. This is good, as it encourages members to come again for more, and is better than providing them with more than they want and giving them spiritual or mental indigestion.

Session Seven
Preparation

If the programme the leader has planned proves to be unrealistic, and there is no chance of completing it, it is better to miss out a whole section and explain that that is what you are doing rather than rush through everything, leaving people with the feeling that nothing has been covered thoroughly.

Careful timing is important, and the temptation to carry on another quarter of an hour should be avoided. Some members may appreciate it, but others may be ready for a change, or may need to be home at a given time.

Sections can be summarized very quickly, with an explanation that they have not been dealt with in depth, but that the overview is meant to put the rest into context.

Planning the timetable of a meeting is difficult and leaders only become proficient at it with practice. Even then it can sometimes come adrift.

Starting and finishing on time is important if the group is to feel purposeful.

9. Too much time

In case the subject is completed more quickly than expected, have something else ready to discuss. It may be helpful to discuss progress to date, or to what extent the group is meeting the aims it has set itself, or ideas for a future programme.

10. The group becomes too big

This is an encouraging problem! It is tempting to keep on growing, and do nothing about it, but once a group regularly has more than fifteen attending, the dynamic changes and some needs are not met.

When all are agreed that the group is too big, you will have to take action.

At one meeting split into two sections, each with a leader, and spend part of the time meeting separately and part of the time together. If it is possible to use another room that helps: if not, go to different parts of the same room.

At the next meeting, do the same thing, keeping the same people in the separated groups where possible, and meet separately for longer.

After three or four meetings like this, suggest that one group meets at a different house, but in a month arrange that all meet together again.

In this way a group can gradually and relatively painlessly divide into two – or multiply into two! Eventually the two groups will have developed an entity of their own and the process may be repeated whenever necessary.

In order to achieve this the leader needs to do some forward planning. There should be an assistant or co-leader working with the leader for some time, ready to take over the second group when necessary; and plans should be made for a second venue so that when the time comes the second group has somewhere to go.

Subsequently the original leader needs to keep some links with the second group, but allow the new leader to become established as leader.

If the two groups both have a new leader, the original leader can simply have a watching brief and will be free to go and start a new group somewhere else! This prevents either of the groups feeling deprived in any way because the other group has the 'real' leader.

11. The group becomes too small

People move away, take on other commitments, or simply lose interest.

When a group regularly has less than six members it can become difficult. If it only ever had five members there is no problem but if it once had twelve or more, there is a sense of failure within the group when it decreases.

There comes a time to say that the group has outlived its useful life, and should be disbanded. This can be painful especially if the group has met together for a long time. Members may be slotted into another group, but they may take some time to settle and may long for the old days. The leader needs to be aware of this and spend time if possible with each one to help them through the period.

It may be possible to increase the group to a viable size simply by asking others to join. Very often people in the church have wondered about joining existing groups but have not quite liked to go along. A personal invitation may be all they need.

Changing the image of a group may be a help. For instance advertising a six-week course on 'Women in the church' or 'Paul's teaching about the cross' or 'Food shortages and our response' may attract new people. Beginning something new gives people an opportunity to join without feeling they are intruding.

Merging two groups which for one reason or another have ceased to be viable can be effective if done sensitively. The two leaders should work together for a while if possible so that neither group feels it has been taken over by the other.

12. *Other problems*

There are other problems which can arise, some of them unique. The good leader will anticipate them and will cope as they arise. Constant review of aims and objectives, and a pastoral concern for each of the members, will keep the leader on the right lines whatever sudden problems arise.

Summary

1. Using handouts, describe problems and consider together how to handle them
2. Using handouts, discuss how to get a group talking
3. Group exercises

1. *Using a handout, describe the problems*

Issue a handout with the problems listed, leaving room for trainees to write notes under each. See page 71, which can be copied.

After you have described each problem either give a brief account of how to handle it, or ask trainees in buzz groups to discuss how to handle it. Briefly share findings.

Ask for other problems encountered in group, and discuss.

2. *Using a handout, discuss how to get a group talking*

Hand out and discuss the 'Hints on how to get a group talking' on page 72.

3. *Group exercises*

Exercise 1 Questionnaire

Aim: To help trainees to anticipate problems and gain experience in deciding how to deal with them.

Method: Hand out to trainees a copy of the questionnaires on page 73. Working on their own or in twos and threes, the trainees fill in the questionnaires. If they are working together, encourage free discussion, but individual decision making.

Have a show of hands for As, Bs and Cs on each question. Ask for any other suggested answers.

Exercise 2 Fishbowl demonstration of good leadership

Aims: To demonstrate how a good leader enables a group to function well; to draw together all the threads of the training course, including styles of leadership, group climate, suitable content and method for the group, coping with problems as they arise.

Method: The trainer becomes leader of a small group, using trainees as group members.

The trainer and six volunteers sit in a small circle in the centre of the room, with the remaining trainees around in a larger circle as observers.

The observers are handed pieces of paper on which to write down their observations.

They draw a circle and indicate by initial letter of name the position of each of the seven people in the small group in the middle.

Each time anyone speaks, the observer puts a tick by that person's initial.

If the remark is addressed to anyone in particular, an arrow goes from the speaker to the person addressed.

If the remark is not relevant to the discussion the tick is crossed. Asides or whispers should be drawn outside the circle. The end result may look something like this.

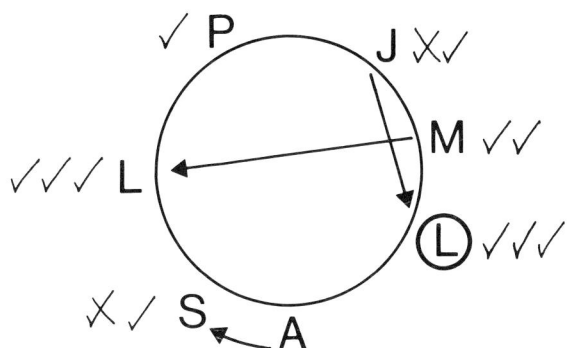

The trainer may lead a discussion on any subject. The suggestion which follows is based on the Parable of the Prodigal Son.

Bible-based discussion on the Prodigal Son (Luke 15. 11–32)

This is a well-known story and in this training situation we can assume that all members have read it before.

The leader opens with a prayer that the Lord will teach us something new from a familiar story; that he will help us not to be self conscious in this rather unnatural situation with people watching, but lead us to be open to each other and to him.

1. Note verses 1 & 2. The context. The hearers of the parable were (*a*) sinners and outcasts (*b*) scribes and Pharisees.
   Think about the story as they heard and applied it.
2. In twos, take a character from the story – father, younger son, elder son – and discuss for two or three minutes how he felt at each stage.
   Leader remains silent during this.
3. Listen to each pair's account of the feeling at each stage in the story. Discuss.
4. Ask: Who does the father in the story represent? The younger son? The elder son?
   Write the three on a chart, one below the other, and at the side write the suggested answers.
5. Ask: Who would the sinners and outcasts identify with within the story? How would it make them feel?
   Who would the scribes and Pharisees identify with? How would it make them feel?
6. Ask: What do we learn about God from this story? What can we learn about ourselves?
   On a chart, list the ideas.
7. What is the application of this story for us?
8. Why did Jesus tell the story? Why did he leave it unfinished?
9. What do you think happened next? Discuss this and follow the discussion with a short role play.
10. Is there a better title than the usual Prodigal Son? Forgiving Father? Two Sons? Any other?
11. Close with prayer, drawing together what has been learned.

Session Seven
Presentation

70 *After the discussion*, look together at the observers' sheets. Notice how many people took part, who spoke most, to whom most remarks were addressed, how many irrelevant comments occurred.

Discuss the *style of leadership*.

Identify *methods* used and discuss whether they were the best for the situation.

What problems arose, and how were they dealt with?

Did the group members feel accepted and respected and comfortable?

What more could have been done?

As a summary of the training course include as many areas as possible in the de-briefing of this group discussion.

Finally pray together, offering the whole of the training course to God. Invite trainees to pray specifically either aloud or in silence about the groups they lead or hope to lead.

Send them out with a commissioning prayer.

Duration of session seven: 80–100 minutes.

Problems a leader might face

1. Too talkative member

2. The silent group

3. Red herrings

4. Difficult questions

5. Arguments

6. Troublemakers

7. Uninterested members

8. Shortage of time

9. Too much time

10. The group becomes too big

11. The group becomes too small

12. Other

Some hints on how to get a group talking

1. It can be helpful to have two leaders. If two people are taking part others are more likely to join in. People may not like to interrupt a monologue, but will join in a conversation. One of the two leaders can ask subsidiary questions or make relevant comments, or fill in a bit of background information.

2. Be informal. A solemn lecture followed by a heavy question is not likely to produce much response. A conversational tone, giving the impression that this is something you have just thought of (though really you have prepared it thoroughly beforehand) will encourage conversation.

3. Do not insist that all remarks are addressed to you. Provided it does not get out of hand, a conversation between other members of the group can be helpful and sometimes you will be well advised to leave them to get on with it, and not inhibit them by dominating the discussion.

4. At the beginning of the meeting hand out slips of paper with Bible references on, or newspaper cuttings, and at the appropriate point in the discussion ask the holder to read it out. Many people will gladly read something that is provided for them and are more likely to be brave enough to voice their own thoughts subsequently once they have made their own voice heard.

5. A shy person can be asked to read a verse in their particular translation if it is one which throws light on the subject. Translations can be provided for this purpose.

6. In a group of ten or more it can be helpful to ask a question and ask people to discuss it with their neighbour for two minutes before sharing their ideas with the whole group. This can help members to clarify their own thinking and give them confidence to address the larger group.

7. In a very large group, of eighteen or more, provide a question and ask people initially to get into twos and discuss it. After two minutes, ask each pair to find another pair to share their thoughts on the question, and on a further question. After five minutes ask each foursome to discuss another question with another four making groups of eight. In this way, everyone gets talking.

Questionnaire on handling problems in groups

In the following situations tick, A, B, or C according to what you would do. If you have any other suggestions, write them at D.

1. In your group one member insists on answering all the questions. Do you:

A Tell him to shut up.
B Speak to him quietly afterwards.
C Let him carry on.
D

2. No one will talk in your group meetings. Do you:

A Disband the group.
B Complain to the minister.
C Go on a training course for group leaders.
D

3. Your group members only want discussion at an intellectual level and they are not prepared to talk about their feelings or take any risks in the group. Do you:

A Spend part of one meeting finding out what they want from the group.
B Keep the discussion as intellectual as possible.
C Only ask questions about what people feel and never about what they think.
D

4. Two of your members like a good gossip and are always making destructive personal remarks about other people in the church. Do you:

A Rebuke them in the meeting, saying it is not Christian to gossip.
B Have a Bible study on the use of the tongue.
C Point out people's good points whenever any criticisms are made.
D

5. Your group is getting smaller because some members have moved away and some have simply stopped coming. Do you:

A Disband the group and encourage members to join another one.
B Ask each member to bring someone with them next time.
C Put up a notice at church saying you have vacancies.
D

SESSION EIGHT
A Resources Evening

This session differs from the other seven in that the trainees will take the initiative by accumulating as much information as they want from what is made available.

The trainer will be on hand to answer questions, and may begin the session with a brief account of what the resources are.

How to set it up

- Collect as many resources for small groups as you can and make a display.

    As well as your own books, catalogues, audio-visuals etc, borrow from anywhere you can, and make use of 'sale or return' facilities from local bookshops or church book agents. Send for catalogues from the agencies listed in the Appendix.
- Group and label the resources to make an easy-to-follow display. Groupings may be:
    - the theory of groups
    - ready-made, ready-to-use study outlines
        for Bible study
        for discussion
    - work books, where every group member has a copy
        for Bible study
        for discussion
    - books to discuss
        on questions of faith
        on questions of practice
    - overseas and Third World subjects
    - special issues
    - evangelistic etc.

- If possible demonstrate soundstrips, videos, audio cassettes.
- Have an area where trainees can practise using videos and projectors. Have cassettes ready to load, filmstrips ready to put in a projector, blank transparencies for trainees to practise with the OHP, large sheets of paper for them to practise writing on wall charts etc.
- Have a table for free literature
- Have a table with copies of this training course in case they want to buy it!
- Include anything which will enable trainees to go away and make an even better job of leading their groups.
- Some churches or groups of churches are building up a resource library of housegroup material which can be borrowed. This is to be encouraged. It needs to be kept up-to-date and the use of it promoted by an enthusiast.

Session Eight
Preparation

RESOURCES APPENDIX

1. *Background reading about theory and practice in small groups*

Baumohl, A., *Making Adult Disciples*, Scripture Union 1984
Copley, T., *Home Bible Studies and How To Run Them*, Paternoster Press 1972/1976
Cotterell, P., *All About Housegroups*, Kingsway 1985
Evans, P., *What? Me A Housegroup Leader?* Grove 1984
Finney, J. *Groups: Asking The Right Questions*, Grove 1984
Hestenes, .\., *Using The Bible In Groups*, Bible Society 1983
Haydon-Knowell, R., *Wednesday Night At Eight*, Kingsway 1985
Haydon-Knowell, R., *How To Lead A Housegroup*, Coastlands 1984
Mallison, J., *Building Small Groups*, Scripture Union 1978
Mallison, J., *Creative Ideas For Small Groups*, Scripture Union 1978
Milson, F., *Small Groups For Christians*, Methodist Church, Division of Education & Youth
Pierson, L., *Ready To Serve*, Scripture Union 1986
Wollen, A. J., *God At Work In Small Groups*, Scripture Union 1983

Available from the Church Pastoral Aid Society are:
Are you sitting uncomfortably?: A soundstrip
Not me, Lord: a 4-week course in group leadership, including 2 audio cassettes
Open House Magazine: published 3 times a year for house group leaders

2. *Bible background and commentaries*

Peake's Commentary on the Bible (one volume), Nelson 1962
The New Bible Commentary (one volume), IVP 1970
The Hodder Bible Handbook, Hodder 1984
The Lion Handbook to the Bible, Lion 1973
The Daily Study Bible (individual volumes), St Andrew Press
The New Century Bible (individual volumes), Oliphants
The Oxford Bible Atlas, OUP ^{2}1974
Using the Bible (a series of 12 volumes), Bible Society
Etienne Charpentier, *How to Read the Old Testament*, SCM Press 1982
　　　　　　　　How to Read the New Testament, SCM Press 1982

Daily Bible reading aids are produced by:
The Bible Reading Fellowship
The International Bible Reading Association
Scripture Union

3. *Ready-to-use outlines for discussion groups*

Anstey, J., *Caring and Sharing*, Albatross 1982
Dawson, R., *Whose Church Is It Anyway?*, British Council of Churches 1986
Foster, R., *Study Guide for Celebration of Discipline*, Hodder 1983
Foster, R., *Study Guide for Money, Sex and Power*, Hodder 1986
Law, M., *Jesus Then and Now Workbook*, Lion 1983
Law, M., *What Christians Believe Workbook*, Lion 1984
Little, P., *Leader's Guide to Know Why You Believe*, Victor 1979
Little, P., *Leader's Guide to Know What You Believe*, Victor 1979
Matthews, J., *Baptism, Eucharist and Ministry – Study Outline*, British Council of Churches 1982
Packer, J. I., *Study Guide: Knowing God*, Hodder 1975
Pierson, L., *Issues facing Christians Today Study Guide* Church Pastoral Aid Society 1986
Pritchard, J. & Simmonds, J., *Travelling Along*, SCM Press 1982
Reardon, M., *What on Earth is the Church for?*, British Council of Churches 1986
Reith, A., *Finding Faith Workbook*, Lion 1984
Watson D., *I Believe in the Church* (study guide), Hodder 1982
Wooderson, M., *Good News Down the Street*, Grove 1982

Learning All Together: Sunday School material for all ages, published 4 times a year by Scripture Union.

Partners in Learning: Sunday School material for all ages, published 3 times a year by the National Christian Education Council.

4. *Ready-to-use outlines for Bible study groups*

These outlines provide background information and discussion questions based on Bible passages. Among the many organizations producing them are:

Bible Reading Fellowship
A sample pack published in 1980, includes a number of separate leaflets, eg *Parables for Parishes, The Great Feast, Guidelines for Missions, Marriage and the Family, Loneliness, Man's Future, Learning to Pray, Worship, Stewardship, Salvation, Faith, Kingdom, Genesis 1–11, Isaiah 40*.
Jones, J., *Following Jesus*, is a discipleship course designed for young people.

Bible Society
Beasley-Murray, P., *To Encourage You*, 1980. 6 studies on I Peter.
Bebbington, E., *The Maker's Instructions*, 1986. 6 studies on the Ten Commandments.
Belben, J. (ed), *Jigsaw Series: Group Bible Studies*, 1986. For 18–30 age group. Titles are: *Understanding New Testament Letters Today, Old Testament Prophets, The Gospels, Old Testament History, Law, Poetry and Wisdom Literature*.
Cooke, F., *Your Light Must Shine*, 1981. 6 studies on The Sermon on the Mount.
Cooke, F., *Please God*, 1979. 10 studies on 'Your kingdom come'.
Frost, R., *Conversation Starters*, 1983. For young people.
Frost, R., *Big Questions*, 1983. For young people.
Grigor, J., *Connections*, 1985. 4 titles: *Building Relationships, Work Relationships, Family Relationships, Challenging Relationships*.
Nilson, M. Y., *Real Living*: an in-depth group study of Luke's Gospel.
Nilson, M. Y., *Steps to Faith*: 3 booklets, each with 10 studies for enquirers and new Christians – *First Steps to Faith, First Steps in Faith, Further Steps in Faith*.
Wade, N., *Action Based on Faith*, 1983. 6 studies on Romans.
Wright, N., *You are my God*, 1982. 6 studies on Psalms 113–118.

Bible Studies, 1985. Each title in the series includes material for 4 or 5 meetings: *Learning about Five Men, Learning from Four Women, Prayer – Learning Together, Faith, Guidance, Say Something Nice for a Change, The Holy Spirit – Who is He?, Studies in the Letter of James, Simple Bible Studies in Luke's Gospel.*

World Council of Churches

Images of Life, 1983. 7 studies on biblical images, including leader's notes and visual aids.

5. *Work books for discussion and Bible study groups*

These differ from outlines for leaders in that each member of the group has a copy and there are usually spaces for writing comments. Among organizations producing them are:

Bible Society

Explore Philippians, 1979. 8 studies.
Explore Amos, 1979. 9 studies.

Methodist Publishing House

E. D. Graham, *Exploring, Deciding, Joining*. 1986. Published for the Methodist Church Membership Committee.

Scripture Union

Coleman, L. & Rydberg, D., *Serendipity Youth Series*, 1984. A series of 9 student books and 3 leader's manuals. *Leader's Guide 1* covers student books *Starters – On Becoming a Christian, Knowing Me – On My Identity, X Certificate – On Moral Questions; Leader's Guide 2* covers student books *Torn Between – On My Lifestyle, Belonging – On Deep Friendships, The Way Ahead – On Discipleship; Leader's Guide 3* covers student books *Hassles – On Relationships, Frontline – On Tough Issues, Directions – On What I Believe.*

Serendipity Bible Studies for Small Groups, 1985/86. Titles include: *Basics, I Believe, Old Testament, From God with Love, I Thought I Knew Him, The Future Starts Here, Don't Give In, Must Get Changed, Look Out, How Human Can You Get?, Just Living, Are You Together?*

For young people's groups, 4 titles by B. Moffet can be recommended: *Power Pack 1* and *Power Pack 2*, each Scripture Union 1986; *Crowdbreakers* and *Crowdmakers*, Marshall Pickering 1983 and 1985. Also F. Goodland, *Over 300 Games for All Occasions*, Scripture Union 1979.

In addition, papers produced by the Methodist Association of Youth Clubs offer helpful material, eg *Sexuality under Discussion, Peace Pack, Race Pack, Life Begins, Partners, Hope for the Best, Other Faiths in Britain, Glimmer of Hope, Helping Others.*

6. *Books to discuss*

Out of the thousands of books which can profitably be discussed in small groups the following are suggested as a start:

Barlow, G. (ed), *Video Violence and Children*, Hodder 1985
Bonhoeffer, D., *Letters and Papers from Prison: An Abridged Edition*, SCM Press 1981
Brooks, P., *Communicating Conviction*, Epworth Press 1983
Buckingham, H., *How to be a Christian in Trying Circumstances*, Epworth Press, 1985
Collinson, N., *The Opening Door*, Epworth Press 1986
Collinson, N. & Matthews, D., *Facing Illness*, Epworth Press, 1986
Gill, R., *The Cross Against The Bomb*, Epworth Press 1984
Hooker, M., *The Message of Mark*, Epworth Press 1983
Hooker, M., *Pauline Pieces*, Epworth Press, 1979

78 Leslie, S., *Children Growing Up*, Scripture Union 1982
Maddocks, N., *The Christian Healing Ministry*, SPCK 1981
Morris, C., *A Week in the Life of God*, Epworth Press 1986
Porter, D., *Children at Risk*, Kingsway 1986
Priestland, G., *Priestland's Progress*, BBC Publications 1981
Richardson, N., *Was Jesus Divine?*, Epworth Press 1979
Sangster, W. E., *The Path to Perfection*, Epworth Press 1943/84
Sharp, M., *What Do We Really Want for Our Children?*, Epworth Press 1986
Sheppard, D., *Bias to the Poor*, Hodder 1980
Smith, J., *A Pocket Guide to Christian Belief*, Mowbray 1986
Taylor, J. V., *The Go-Between God*, SCM Press 1972
Thomas, J. H., *The Pilgrim's Progress in Today's English*, Kingsway 1979
Tournier, P., *Creative Suffering*, SCM Press 1982
Townsend, M., *Our Tradition of Faith*, Epworth Press 1980
Tutu, D., *Crying in the Wilderness*, Mowbray 1986
Ward, N., *The Use of Praying*, Epworth Press, 1967
Watson, D., *Discipleship*, Hodder 1981
Wiltsher, C., *Everyday Science, Everyday God*, Epworth Press 1986
Winwood, D., *I Want to Begin a Christian Life*, Methodist Church Division of Education & Youth 1983
Young, F., *Face to Face*, Epworth Press 1985

7. *Audio-visual aids*

Books about AVA

Griggs, *Using the Bible with Audio-Visual Aids*, Bible Society 1980
Lazell, D., *Know How to use Video*, Scripture Union 1985
    Help! I Can't Draw: Books 1, 2, 3, Kingsway
    Guide to Christian Video, Jay Books 1986
    (a comprehensive catalogue)
    See for Yourself, Jay Books 1986
    (how to choose and use video cassettes)

Organizations which produce and supply AVA
Anchor Recordings
Bible Society
Bible Today Ltd
Concord Film Council Ltd
Concordia Filmstrips
Church Army Communications Unit
Church Pastoral Aid Society
CTVC Film and Video Library
Christian Video Experience
Lion Publishing (Overhead Projection Materials)
Scripture Union

Most of the above will supply catalogues on request. Some religious bookshops sell and hire out films, soundstrips and video cassettes.

8. *Dance, Drama, Mime and Music*

General
Beall, P. & Keys, M., *The Folk Arts in God's Family*, Hodder 1983

Beall, P., *Growing Together in God's Family*, Celebration 1983
Hinton, J., *Open Family*, Celebration 1983

Drama
Burbridge, P., *Time to Act*, Hodder 1979
Burbridge, P. & Watts, M., *Red Letter Days*, Hodder 1986
Grace, F., *Back to Back's Little Paper Back Book*, Kingsway 1985
Grainger, R., *Presenting Drama in Church*, Epworth Press 1985
Grinham, G., *Know How to Use Drama in Church*, Scripture Union 1979
Maggs Video Services, *Act One*, Maggs 1984
Maggs Video Services, *Act Two*, Maggs 1984
Maggs Video Services, *Act Three*, Maggs 1985
Martin, A. & Kelso, A., *Scene One*, Kingsway 1986
Stickley, S. & Belben, J., *Using the Bible in Drama*, Bible Society 1980
Watts, M., *Lightning Sketches*, Hodder 1981
Watts, M., *Laughter in Heaven*, Marc Europe 1985

Dance
Blogg, M., *Dance and the Christian Faith*, Hodder 1985
Challingsworth, N., *Liturgical Dance Movement*, Mowbray 1982
Davies, J. G., *Liturgical Dance*, SCM Press 1984
Lamont, G. &. R., *Move It*, Bible Society 1981
Lamont, G. &. R., *Move Yourselves*, Bible Society 1983
Stevenson G. &. J., *Steps of Faith*, Kingsway 1984

Music
Kendrick, G., *Worship*, Kingsway 1984
Maries, A., *Using the Bible in Music*, Bible Society 1983
Maries, A., *One Heart One Voice*, Hodder 1985

9. *Addresses*

Amnesty International, British Section, 5 Roberts Place, Off Bowling Green Lane, London EC1 0EJ
Anchor Recordings, 72 The Street, Kennington, Ashford, Kent TN24 9HS
British Council of Churches, Edinburgh House, 2 Eaton Gate, London SW1W 9BL
Bible Today, Ashwood, 6 Pembroke Road, Northwood, Middlesex HA6 2HR
Bible Society, Stonehill Green, Westlea, Swindon SN5 7DG
Bible Reading Fellowship, St Michael's House, 2 Elizabeth Street, London SW1W 9RQ
Care Trust (Christian Action Research and Education), 21a Down Street, London W1Y 7DN
Christian Aid, 240–250 Ferndale Road, London SW9 8BH
Christian World Centre, PO Box 30, 123 Deansgate, Manchester M60 3BX
Church Army Communications Unit and Resource Centre, Winchester House, Independents Road, Blackheath, London SE3 9LF
Church Pastoral Aid Society, Falcon Court, 32 Fleet Street, London EC4Y 1DB
Crusade for World Revival, PO Box 11, Walton-on-Thames, Surrey KT12 1BD
Concord Films Council Ltd, 201 Felixstowe Road, Ipswich, Suffolk 1PR 9BJ
Concordia Filmstrips, 18 Cranes Way, Borehamwood, Herts WD6 2EU
Christian Video Experience, 2 Cecil Way, Hayes, Bromley, Kent BR2 7JU
CTVC Film and Video Library, Beesons Yard, Bury Lane, Rickmansworth, Herts.
Celebration Services Ltd, 57 Dorchester Road, Lytchett Minster, Poole, Dorset BH16 6JE
Deo Gloria Outreach, 7 London Road, Bromley, Kent BR1 1BZ

80 Divisions of the Methodist Church: Home Missions, Social Responsibility Ministries; 1 Central Buildings, Westminster, London SW1H 9NR
Overseas Division, 25 Marylebone Road, London NW1 5JR
Division of Education and Youth, 2 Chester House, Pages Lane, Muswell Hill, London N10 1PR
Epworth Press: All books obtainable from SCM Bookroom
Evangelical Alliance, 186 Kennington Park Rd, London SE1W 9LZ
International Bible Reading Association, Robert Denholm House, Nutfield, Redhill, Surrey RH1 4HW
Methodist Publishing House, Wellington Road, Wimbledon, London SW19 8EU
National Christian Education Council, Robert Denholm House, Nutfield, Redhill, Surrey RH1 4HW
Scripture Union, 130 City Road, London EC1V 2NJ
SCM Press and SCM Bookroom, 26–30 Tottenham Road, London N1 4BZ

It is proposed that this Appendix should be brought up to date every two years. Copies can be obtained from the Division of Ministries of the Methodist Church, 1 Central Buildings, Westminster, London SW1H 9NR. There may be a small charge.